P9-DOA-514

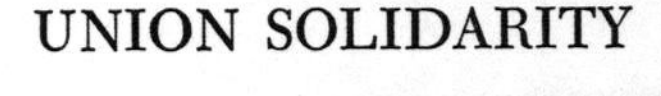

UNION SOLIDARITY

Union Solidarity

THE INTERNAL COHESION OF A LABOR UNION

BY

Arnold M. Rose

THE UNIVERSITY OF MINNESOTA PRESS · MINNEAPOLIS
LONDON · GEOFFREY CUMBERLEGE · OXFORD UNIVERSITY PRESS

PRINTED AT THE NORTH CENTRAL PUBLISHING COMPANY, ST. PAUL

Library of Congress Catalog Card Number: 52-5322

Foreword

Most of those interested in the relations between labor and management have tended to regard "labor" as one of two things: (1) the abstract unit of production which the economist studies or (2) the concrete unit of collective bargaining – the union – which the industrial relations expert studies. Labor is another thing also, if it is not too obvious to point out; it is a group of human beings who have certain needs and interests. The union, even if it is completely undemocratic in organization, aims to satisfy those needs or express those interests. Ultimately the union is strong or is weak depending on the attitudes of its members toward it. An understanding of the role of the union in labor relations cannot be complete without an understanding of the motivations and attitudes of the workers behind the union. Yet labor economists and industrial relations experts, despite much worthy research and analysis, have thus far unfortunately had to rely on certain assumptions about internal relationships within the bodies of men known as "labor" or "management," except in terms of formal structure. But little effort has yet been made to test these assumptions.[1] The present study

[1] This point concerning the lack of internal studies of management is made by Melville Dalton, "Conflicts between Staff and Line Managerial Officers," *American Sociological Review*, XV (June 1950), 342. The lack of studies on the internal relations and operations of the union has been noted by the following writers: (1) Wilbert Moore, "Industrial Sociology: Status and Prospects," *American Sociological Review*, XIII (August 1948), 382, 386; (2) C. W. M. Hart, "Industrial Relations Research and Social Theory,"

illustrates how this gap in our knowledge can be filled, and how important it is to fill it. Unfortunately, it is only an illustration, for it is a study of only one local union (albeit a local of more than 8,500 members). Few unions are exactly alike, and the union we are studying probably is far from average or typical either in its history or in its role in industrial organization. The mere fact, for example, that this union operates in a field which is only partly unionized, and with a wide variety of employers, gives it a character that a union in a mass production field with only one or two employers does not have. Hence no generalizations can be drawn which apply to the whole union movement. Nevertheless, the attitudes of the workers in this union, as reported in this study, will carry some lesson to many persons interested in unions. Some observers are cynical, others are idealistic, about the rank-and-file members of the unions. A study of the facts about even one union should correct both of those extreme viewpoints.[2]

Canadian Journal of Economics and Political Science, XV (February 1949), 53, 56.

The following authors have made first steps toward studies of internal union relationships: (1) Herbert A. Shephard, "Democratic Control in a Labor Union," *American Journal of Sociology*, LIV (January 1949), 311–315; (2) C. Wright Mills, "What Does a UAW Member Look Like?" *UAW–CIO Ammunition*, VI (August 1948), 30–33; (3) E. Wight Bakke and Clark Kerr, *Union Management and the Public* (New York: Harcourt, 1948); (4) Theodore Newcomb, "Labor Unions as Seen by Their Members: An Attempt to Measure Attitudes," in *Industrial Conflict: A Psychological Interpretation*, edited by G. W. Hartmann and T. Newcomb (New York: Cordon Co., 1939), pp. 313–338.

A much more thorough study was initiated independently and almost simultaneously with ours by the Survey Research Center at the University of Michigan. The findings of their last-named study were not available at the time of publication of this book, but they should be of great interest in suggesting the generalizability of findings, since the two studies are of quite dissimilar unions. Our schedule is currently being used as one of the bases for gathering information in a study being conducted at the University of Chicago. It is hoped that other similar studies may be made, and to that end the schedule and criticisms of it are presented in Appendix II.

[2] Lest we appear to exaggerate the differences between our union and a union in a mass production industry, we should point out that workers in a distribution field, like workers in a mass production field, realize that they are easily replaceable by an employer. The most important industrial characteristic of the workers studied in this monograph is that they are unskilled, a trait they share with the majority of contemporary workers.

The study raises three questions of general concern to most persons interested in the labor movement: (1) For what reasons can workers feel a sense of solidarity with their union? (2) To what extent can union leaders and union experiences educate the rank and file to have attitudes considered by the leaders to be essential for successful trade unionism? (3) To what extent can a union buck a strong cultural pattern of which their members are a part when this opposition is deemed necessary for union solidarity and successful union operation? Accordingly, Chapter III (coming after two chapters forming an introduction to the problem of the study and to its method) deals with the general question of participation and loyalty. Chapter IV answers several questions on the extent to which members agree with various aspects of union policy. Chapter V considers the difficult matter of race prejudice and the union's role in intergroup relations. Subsequent chapters take up differences between various groups of members and draw theoretical and practical conclusions from the whole investigation.

The idea for the study was originally that of Harold J. Gibbons, director of Teamsters Local 688. After conferring with several persons, including me, he requested the American Jewish Committee, through Dr. Samuel H. Flowerman of the Committee's Scientific Department, to undertake the study. The Committee generously agreed, provided that half the estimated expense would be paid by the union. (Later the Committee provided another small amount to pay for some of the additional costs of the study.) It was agreed that the present author was to do the study without compensation.

I wish to thank Dr. Flowerman not only for securing funds for the study but also for his valued suggestions for and criticisms of the original schedule and the final manuscript. As one of the expert critics, Dr. Flowerman helped to bring the report up to whatever quality it may claim.

One of the unusual characteristics of Teamsters Local 688 of St. Louis was manifested in its willingness to undertake the study. Few organizations of any kind are willing to open themselves to scrutiny by an outsider, even if he is considered to be an impartial scientist, and few organizational leaders are willing to allow the success of their policies to be measured. This union's leaders recognized the need to understand better the attitudes of the rank and file toward all policies and invited the author to undertake this study. The overwhelming majority of the rank-and-file members cooperated freely in interviews because they felt that the union would be able to improve itself from the study's conclusions. A book of this sort, available to the general public, was not envisaged when the study was begun, but the investigator was accorded a free hand to look into what he would and to write up the findings in any manner he chose. These things required courage on the part of the union's leaders, as anyone who knows the precarious inner structure of a conflict organization realizes. Wisdom and courage thus are demonstrated to be characteristics of Director Harold J. Gibbons and the Stewards' Council of Local 688.

This does not mean that there was no opposition to the study when it was proposed by Director Gibbons to his staff and to the Stewards' Council (which is the legislative arm of the union, elected directly by the rank and file). The proposal came shortly after the public opinion polls failed to predict the outcome of the 1948 elections, and some stewards were dubious about the whole questionnaire-interview approach. They felt that their personal contacts with the rank-and-file members over a long period of time gave them more insight into members' attitudes than any outsider – especially a college professor who could not be expected to understand the problems workers face – exploring the anatomy of their union.

It was a warm discussion, but the open attitudes that all democratic leaders have at least as part of their make-up, as well as the charismatic quality of Gibbons' persuasiveness, prevailed, and the study was approved. Minor though it is, this act is certainly one of the most dramatic manifestations of democracy, courage, and open-mindedness in the annals of union history.

Next to Gibbons, Carl Leathwood of the union staff was of the greatest aid in the operations of the study. The author was also aided on question selection and member location by the following members of the staff of the union: Bernice Fisher, Leon Higginbotham, Arthur Johnson, Richard Kavener, Phil Reichardt, Pete Saffo, George Seiler, and Barney Trefts. Annette Dieckmann of the St. Louis Labor Education Project was helpful with criticisms of the questionnaire and the first draft of the report. Eleanor Coit of the American Labor Education Service is remembered gratefully for encouraging the idea of the study.

Since the total funds available for the study were severely limited, a good deal of free labor had to be provided by the author and his students. I was fortunate enough to have five enthusiastic students in my course on Public Opinion Research at Washington University who helped at several stages of the work. They are Lois Abrams, Harry V. Ball, Ann Faust, Henry P. Outten, and Arthur E. Prell. Miss Abrams and Mr. Ball also undertook special assignments as part of the paid staff. My wife, Caroline B. Rose, undertook the arduous task of editing all completed questionnaires, and served as a valued critic of the first draft of the manuscript. Students in undergraduate courses at Washington University aided in the interviewing. Students who undertook one or more interviews include:

Erwin Abram	Joann Gutridge	Melba Leichsenring
Louis Armstrong	Robert Hagen	Robert Lyng
William P. Barth	Ione Hedges	Herbert Meikle
Mary L. Bender	Betty K. Hibbeler	Lawrence Milstead
J. F. W. Clark	William Hykins	Frankie Love
Ellen Cone	Fred Koenig	Eugene O'Brien
Lawrence L. Coulon	Edele Kooreman	Charles R. Oldham
Albert S. DeNuzzio	Robert Kleinschmidt	Don Perry
Edwin Fixler	Ray Lartz	Ruth Raymond
Frank E. Goetz	Saul Lassoff	Robert Reed
Barbara Grove	Barbara Lippert	Dorothy Rich

David Richmond	Joyce Sievers	Rudolph Torini
Raymond W. Rosenthal	Eleanor Smith	Minette Van Berg
Dorothy Saunders	Dorothy J. Sparks	Mabel B. Ward
Maurice Schwartz	Harold St. Gemme	James West
William M. Seward	Robert Terte	John D. Wright
Virgil Seymour	A. L. Thurman	

I wish to express my appreciation also to Andreas Papandreou, economist, and Benjamin Willerman, psychologist – both professors at the University of Minnesota. They read the completed manuscript and made several valuable suggestions for its improvement.

In centuries past, the writing of a book gave a scholar ample opportunity to express himself fully on the nature of the universe and of man. Today scholars have specialized themselves into two groups: those who write theoretical essays and those who write factual reports. While in general it is not supposed to be necessary or even desirable to combine those two functions, occasionally a little deviation occurs. Even the judge – who is supposed solely to "read" (observe and report on) the law – occasionally delivers himself of *obiter dicta.* The scientist is occasionally forgiven for writing an essay. He may even offer some broad improved hypotheses, perhaps even some that are unprovable in terms of accessible knowledge, in the preface to a book – such as the following.

The American labor movement, despite its great age (going back to at least 1820), is a conflict group which has not been found acceptable to most of the nonlabor elements of American society. Yet there are more than 60 million jobholders in a total population of 150 million, and 16 million of them are members of unions. Most of them vote, and thus form a sizable power in, and have a major responsibility for, democratic American society. Their interest in their jobs – that is, in present and future economic security – is one of the most powerful of their interests. Most of them have only one other institutional interest and affiliation – the churches. The organization which best expresses their interest in economic security is the union. This interest is so powerful that the unions will survive as long as there is a democratic political system. We predict, *ex cathedra*, that unions will survive the attacks of uncompromising business leaders, of federal and state legislators, and of racketeering labor leaders.

Yet these unions – ultimately based on so powerful a human interest and having so much potential power in the political system – have little connection with the rest of the institutional structure of the United States. Organizations have a far narrower class composition than most of us realize or care to admit. The unions are the major organizations of the industrial working class, and they have little or no contact with organizations composed of middle- or upper-class people. Take, for example, the League of Women Voters. Despite its nonpartisan, general-social-welfare character, it includes very few women from the two thirds of the population with the lowest incomes. Even the fraternal associations and veterans' organizations have not been able to attract a significant proportion of the working classes: despite their proud boast that they are large and typically "American," they are largely middle class in membership. Formerly one of the blocks to membership in these organizations was the large proportion of the foreign-born among urban workers, but now even though the immigrants are dying off, only a slightly larger proportion of the working class are members of lodges or veterans' groups.

In addition to the distinctive class character of American organizations, there is to be noted a lack of communication between organizations of lower-class composition and those of middle- and upper-class composition. This was perhaps not too surprising when the union movement was small, but now that it is large and the situation has still changed only slightly, it has great significance for the entire social structure and political organization of the United States. It is true that unions are asked to place a representative or two on boards of social welfare or civic reform organizations. But most of these representatives are secretaries of city associations of unions or, at best, directors of the larger locals. They are usually the paid professionals of the labor movement rather than the rank-and-file leaders, and a very few of them are appointed to so many executive boards that they seldom have the time to attend them all. Union contact with the rest of the community through the newspapers is somewhat better, but most newspapers have an economic interest in not being too friendly to unions, and the contact is not a personal one but is transmitted through the refracting medium of reporters and editors.

Numerous problems arise out of the failure of communication between the classes. One is that the middle and upper classes do not understand the drive for security on the part of the workers, or the workers' failure to seek status in middle-class terms. They do not understand why workers value seniority over promotion, prefer social security legislation to reduced taxes, or object to "being bossed." This misunderstanding about social values is probably the most important source of class consciousness and class conflict.

Another problem is political in nature. The working class is becoming interested in politics. As Elmo Roper[3] discovered in an analysis of the 1948 election statistics, the proportion of persons of the lower-income group voting in 1948 increased over that of previous elections, while the proportion of voters of middle and upper incomes declined. Organized labor has taken over political leadership in several American cities and is very close to political dominance in several state governments. Unfortunately, it knows as little about the needs and interests of the middle and upper classes as the latter know of the working class. For example, it does not understand the insecurity of the self-employed or the economic values of the small producer, and may use its political power to drive production and distribution more into the hands of large corporations because it is easier to bargain collectively with a few large employers than with many small ones. Also, the new labor governments do not usually know

[3] Reprint of article in the *New York Herald Tribune*, June 19, 1949.

the techniques for operating certain departments of government with high efficiency. The blunders of Ernest Bevin, a trade union leader who became Britain's foreign minister, are notorious. And—in another setting—a trade union official of Racine, Wisconsin, told me that the union leaders who had won control of the government of that city did not have the background to run effectively a certain important branch of that government.

These are just two of the many problems that arise out of the failure of communication between the classes. Assuming that the direction of our society is not toward the complete liquidation of all those who are not now members of the working class, some efforts to re-establish lines of communication are called for. The present efforts of the press to report labor news can be extended and made more accurate and impartial. The appointment of labor representatives to executive boards of civic and social welfare organizations can be increased and diversified. The now dying efforts of the industrial department of the Y.W.C.A.—carried on for over twenty-five years, sometimes with notable success—to elevate and broaden young leaders of the working class need to be given new life. A successful experiment like that of the League of Women Voters to put on an educational exhibit and program for wives of UAW–CIO members in Detroit should be duplicated by other groups in other cities. The nonprofit grocery operated temporarily by Teamsters Local 688 during a period of unusually high prices, which was made available to interested citizens who were not members of the union, should be re-established on sounder grounds by this and other unions. The efforts of a few unions to explain their actions to the general public via newspaper and radio advertisements should be greatly extended. Among the ways of establishing contact between workers and nonworkers is to write and publicize descriptions of unions and their functions. Hence one reason for this report.

Another reason is to increase communication between union members and union leaders. In various unions there are differing degrees of adequacy in this kind of communication, but in probably no union is it perfect. The leaders fail to communicate perfectly with the members, and the members fail to communicate perfectly with the leaders. Probably the success of communication is a function of democracy in structure and smallness of membership. This study is concerned with the communication from leaders to members insofar as it points out the extent to which, and in what respects, this communication is successful or unsuccessful. Thus in Chapter IV we analyze the degree to which union members accept certain principles which the union leaders deem essential to successful trade unionism. This study is concerned with the communication from members to leaders insofar as it brings to leaders information about members' attitudes. A sizable proportion of the findings of this study were found to be new information to the leaders of Local 688. Studies of the attitudes of their rank and file have been found to be of great value to the leaders of the army and of industry.[4] An aim of our study was to demonstrate a similar value to unions. Both union leaders and individual rank-and-file members should be interested in knowing what their union as a whole is like.

This study has been made possible by the cooperation of all the individuals and groups mentioned in earlier paragraphs. The interpretations are the author's own responsibility.

Arnold M. Rose

University of Minnesota
August 1950

[4] See Samuel A. Stouffer *et al.*, *The American Soldier* (2 vols., Princeton: Princeton University Press, 1949). The whole field of consumer "market" research and industrial relations research has grown up to service industry.

Table of Contents

List of Tables

UNION SOLIDARITY

CHAPTER I

Worker Solidarity and the Local Union

When the Union's inspiration thru the worker's blood shall run,
There can be no greater power anywhere beneath the sun.
Yet what force on earth is weaker than the feeble strength of one?
But the Union makes us strong!
Solidarity forever!
Solidarity forever!
Solidarity forever!
For the Union makes us strong!
It is we who plowed the prairies, built the cities where they trade,
Dug the mines and built the workshops, endless miles of railroad laid.
Now we stand outcast and starving 'mid the wonders we have made.
Solidarity forever!
Solidarity forever!
Solidarity forever!
For the Union makes us strong!

A. The Historical Setting of Worker Solidarity

The anthem of the union movement – sung to the stirring melody of "The Battle Hymn of the Republic" – states some of the premises on which union solidarity is based: (1) that by joining a union, workers can get a larger share of the economic product than they can by individual bargaining,

(2) that by forming a fellowship of the individually powerless, workers can secure a measure of control over the environment that otherwise almost completely controls them. A third premise can be expressed in the terminology of the first item of the 1944 Declaration of the International Labor Organization: "Labour is not a commodity."

For all but highly skilled workers who have a measure of personal irreplaceability, the bargaining power of workers is a function of their solidarity. Solidarity is thus as valuable to the worker as ownership is to the employer. Both provide the power basis on which an agreement is made to combine skills, work, tools, and organization for the common goal of production. Worker solidarity has recently come to mean more than advantages to be exacted from the employer; for some workers it has also come to mean partially coordinated action in politics, collective absorption of the risks of ill health, and some cooperative effort in housing, etc.

In this book we shall limit consideration of labor solidarity to that which is found in a single union. We thereby eliminate any discussion of relationships among workers when these are not expressed in the form of a permanent organization. What is not considered might range from a love of one's fellow men to a strong sense of class consciousness, but it differs from solidarity within a clearly specifiable organization. We also eliminate from consideration a possible feeling of unity among all organized workers, which was the way in which the term solidarity was used by some of the older labor economists.[1] They considered solidarity a quality that was a goal for organized labor. We consider solidarity an existing fact, a feeling that workers have in a certain measure, which can rise and fall depending on the changing strength of several influences.

In a democratic society the existence of a union is evidence that a degree of solidarity exists among its members. If the members joined it in its organizational stages—and

[1] See, for example, Selig Perlman, *A Theory of the Labor Movement* (New York: Macmillan, 1928).

the group that did so includes a large number of present-day American union members because of the phenomenal expansion of unions during the past fifteen years – they must have felt some need for combining forces, which is solidarity. If union membership was imposed on them during the period of the closed shop, workers must still get some of their needs satisfied by the union. Otherwise the unions would have broken up rather than grown stronger when the Taft-Hartley law abolished the closed shop and the compulsion to join a union. Our own study of a single union shows little difference in the answers to questions about basic union loyalty between workers who had voluntarily organized the union and those who had been forced to join an already existing union. In both groups over 90 per cent say they need a union to buck the employer for them, although many are critical of specific aspects of the union's activity and organization.

Satisfying the worker's needs is, then, at least one of the union's goals, both manifest and latent. This viewpoint is accepted not only by partisans of the labor movement, but by labor economists. For example, Neil W. Chamberlain of Yale University's Labor and Management Center describes union goals in terms of members' needs: security for the union and its members, recognition, and self-expression.[2] E. Wight Bakke, director of the same Center, finds from interviews with workers that they join unions in order to satisfy the following needs: (1) the society and respect of other people; (2) the degree of creature comforts and economic security possessed by the most favored of their customary associates; (3) independence in and control over their own affairs; (4) understanding of the forces and factors at work in their world; (5) integrity.[3]

If the union serves these psychological needs, the search

[2] Neil W. Chamberlain, *The Union Challenge to Management Control* (New York: Harper, 1948), pp. 100–111.

[3] E. Wight Bakke, "Why Workers Join Unions," *Personnel*, XXII (July 1945), 37–46.

for the roots of worker solidarity must lead us to an examination of the historical condition out of which the union movement first sprang. We shall take Karl Polanyi,[4] the economic historian, as our guide. He points out that the free enterprise system gives the producer a higher standard of living and lower degree of job security than any other known to either the historian or the anthropologist. The combination of modern technology and competition has produced such a high level of rationalized efficiency in production that the ordinary worker can afford to purchase the full range of necessities and some luxuries as well, and the owners and managers of industry can look forward to accumulations of wealth formerly possessed only by kings and the highest of nobles. At the same time the worker can suddenly lose his job, and the businessman lose his business, because of a technological change or a business depression, so that neither has a great deal of certainty about the future.

In premodern times the serf might exist on a pittance and not even be a free man, but he could not be removed from the land which provided him a basic sustenance (except by disease or crop destruction, which were regarded as acts of God and thus not subject to man's control anyway). The feudal lord might have a bare castle and be fairly restricted in the activities he might engage in or the distance he might safely travel, but he had a self-sustaining village to guarantee his support. The industrial artisan might have to work many years as an apprentice without pay, but his guild protected his occupation from competitors and assured him of a market. Neither lord nor serf nor artisan was subject to the whims of a competitive market, nor could he be threatened by inventions. He had economic security.

The Industrial Revolution and the free market system changed all that. Few men could now be sure of their economic futures: unemployment and business failure were possibilities for everyone. The average rewards were greater, but the occasional penalties were more severe. Furthermore,

[4] *The Great Transformation* (New York: Farrar and Rinehart, 1944).

labor was regarded as a commodity, as a "factor in production." Under these circumstances it was natural for men to try to protect themselves, to reduce the risks, and to increase their power by collective action. The businessmen formed combines to control the market, created corporations to limit their liability in case of failure, entered into agreements to prevent the free use of inventions, distributed their investments so that all would not be likely to go bad at the same time, and paid politicians so that control of natural resources and transportation routes could be assured. Some time afterward, the workers formed or joined unions, set restrictions on job entry, and pressured politicians into voting for minimum wage laws and for old age and unemployment insurance laws.

In the light of history, then, unions can be viewed to some extent as a means of regaining the security, recognition, and self-expression for the worker which had been lost because of the growth of modern capitalism and the Industrial Revolution. Investigators not partial to the labor movement, like Elton Mayo, have emphasized the modern worker's hunger for these things, even though these investigators do not mention the function of the union in satisfying that hunger.[5] If we examine the specific motivations more closely, we can see that even the most undemocratic and corrupt unions do satisfy it in some measure. No union allows an employer to dismiss a worker from his job without sufficient and agreed-upon reasons; at the beginning of depressions some unions insist on spreading out the work; all unions try to enforce a seniority system in promotions and necessary layoffs; many unions try to reduce competition for their members by restricting the labor market; a few unions are working for an

[5] "Trade unions are mentioned twice in Mayo's writings, once when he alludes to the resistance of trade unions to technological change (*Human Problems of an Industrial Civilization*, 1946, p. 181) and a second time when he states that trade unions repeat the mistake of management in organizing for industrial warfare rather than cooperation (*The Political Problem of Industrial Civilization*, 1947, p. 22)." Reinhard Bendix and Lloyd H. Fisher, "The Perspectives of Elton Mayo," *Review of Economics and Statistics*, XXXI, No. 4 (November 1949), 316.

annual wage or use a hiring-hall system to guarantee at least a minimum of work for every member. Some of these measures may make for economic inefficiency; most of them irk many employers; but all of them add to the union member's job security – at least in the short run, when he can see it.[6]

Recognition and self-expression are largely gained for the union member to the extent that he participates in union activities. Only a few unions – and only a few employers – encourage creativity on the job: under conditions of mass production there is little room for creativity. But in the union itself there is some room for self-expression and individual recognition. While some union leaders allow very little or no participation on the part of the rank and file in the actual running of the union, there is more participation of other kinds than most people are aware of. At the lowest level of making routine complaints to the employer in the name of the union, practically all unions allow rank-and-file activity. Many unions encourage rank-and-file members to serve as shop stewards and as members of contract negotiating committees. Many unions, if not most, have ultimate control by election, although it may be extremely difficult to organize an effective opposition on a national basis. Participation on nonpolitical levels is greater than in the political activities

[6] The central importance of job security for workers has been observed by most students of labor. Barbash, for example, says: "If there is one overriding consideration which motivates the unions' attitudes with respect to the terms of the collective agreement it is fear – fear of there not being enough jobs to go around, fear of unjust discharge, and fear of unequal treatment – in short, insecurity. The available evidence on the character of the economic and social order seems to indicate that this fear of insecurity is rather well grounded in the realities of earning a living. During the war, when the elements of economic insecurity in the environment were offset by full employment, many of the practices arising out of this fear reaction were drastically modified. The working conception of society created by this fear reaction on the part of workers and their unions, and which is shared by other economic groups, was perceptively stated a generation ago by a discerning student of labor affairs, Robert Hoxie, who said, 'So far as workers are concerned, there is no society as a whole and no long run but immediate need and rival social groups'." (Jack Barbash, *Labor Unions in Action* [New York: Harper, 1948], p. 99. The source of the Hoxie statement is: International Brotherhood of Electrical Workers, *Wage Trends and Related Subjects* [Washington, 1925], p. 22.)

we have just considered: most unions have a number of social affairs, every member carries a card and usually wears a union button, and he receives the union's literature. Seeing how little the average lower-income adult participates in any other kind of organization,[7] except for his church, what may appear to the outsider as a low amount of participation in the union will to the union member himself seem a high relative amount of participation.

In most unions various symbols are used to create a sense of identification. We have already mentioned the button, which is supposed to be worn while on the job. References to the union on the part of the leaders, in speeches, leaflets, posters, etc., is usually in terms of "*your* union" rather than any of the possible impersonal ways. Union leaders, as well as rank-and-file members, are referred to as "brother so-and-so" no matter how impersonal their relationship to the rank-and-file members. The member is encouraged to look for the union label on products he buys and to observe the actions of certain politicians who he has been told are pro-union men. In such a situation it is likely that the average union member gets a sense of self-expression out of union achievement and is frequently aware of union activity. Having some sense of insignificance and impotence in a complex world, the worker apparently gets some satisfactions out of seeing an organization to which he belongs swinging some weight in the world. Feeling at least somewhat repressed about talking back to the boss, the worker can get vicarious satisfaction when his union—that is, the union staff member or business agent—talks to the boss as an equal.

Most of the cases of friction between employer and employee are trivial, even from the standpoint of the particular industry or union as a whole. But these numerous, trivial grievances are very close to the average union member; even if he does not personally know the worker with the griev-

[7] See, for example, Ira DeA. Reid and Emily L. Ehle, "Leadership Selection in Urban Locality Areas," *Public Opinion Quarterly*, XIV (Summer 1950), 262–284.

ance, he can identify himself with the latter because their situations are likely to be so similar. In the larger controversies between union and management, the conflict may become dramatic and reports of it may appear in the newspaper. To the extent that the individual worker identifies himself with his union, he gains psychological rewards from the union's large-scale activities, and these rewards are in turn a stimulus to further identification. If the union wins a controversy, the average member gains not only in material advantage but also in a sense of achievement. If the union loses, the member has not lost much more than he would have lost if he were never a member of a union, and he has had the psychological satisfaction of having participated in an effort to improve his position. It is likely that even the culturally backward coal miner in an isolated mountain village feels himself to be a participant in a national drama whenever John L. Lewis hits the front pages of the nation's press. Better to be opposed than to be ignored.

With the depersonalization of the employer as a consequence of the rise of the industrial corporation, there is less possibility for the worker to feel sympathy for, or loyalty to, the employer.[8] The modern corporation provides more material rewards for its workers than did the robber baron or honest manufacturer of the nineteenth century, but it is more difficult to credit it with humanitarian motives. The size of the modern corporation and the difficulty of the worker in understanding it encourage him to turn to the union as his negotiator with the company. In this sense the union is like the church: it serves the average worker by interceding for him with the forces that control his world.

Insofar as unions have recently been helping their members by providing legal aid and advice or guidance in voting, in securing unemployment and old age insurance benefits, and in seeking various other social services offered by fed-

[8] The process by which this attitude develops is traced in one factory by W. L. Warner and J. O. Low, *The Social System of the Modern Factory. The Strike: A Social Analysis* (New Haven: Yale University Press, 1947).

eral, state, and local governments,[9] they assist in adjusting the more ignorant workers to the increasing complexities of modern life. It is true that most government services are available without an intermediary. But the worker may not know that, or he may be suspicious of or repelled by the red tape or the impersonal white collar civil servant who asks him all sorts of questions before providing the free public service. If the union directs him how to secure the service and tells him it is harmless to answer all the questions, he will feel happier and be more likely to go through all the steps necessary to get the service.

In writing of the newly formed local of the UAW-CIO for the Ford plant, Weybright reported in 1941: "The corridors of the present building teem all day with members. Some come to visit, most come on business, but scores each day come because it is the friendliest place they know to ask personal questions—how to get a birth certificate, pick a doctor or lawyer, locate an apartment, join an orchestra, get up a ball team, or take a course in dramatics."[10] Many unions thus now perform the same function that the political ward boss did a generation ago: in the eyes of those whom they help, they are doing a little political "fixing"; from the standpoint of the outside observer their services are more modestly seen as guides to a bureaucratic government.

Most unions perform these services haphazardly and incompletely. Some unions do more and others do less, but probably none saturate the worker to the full extent of his felt needs for security, recognition, and self-expression. Especially noteworthy is the decline that occurred in membership participation in the running of the union as the "business union" AF of L philosophy supplanted the populist philosophy of the Knights of Labor, the anarchist philosophy of

[9] In Chicago, and perhaps in other cities, the CIO has organized a recurring course for union staff members where they can learn of the many services provided by government for which their rank-and-file members may be eligible.

[10] Victor Weybright, "Ford Puts on the Union Label," *Survey Graphic*, XXX (November 1941), 555.

the IWW, and the socialist philosophy of the early needle trades' unions.[11] Within the last fifteen years the greater activity of the government in controlling labor relations has also reduced somewhat the possibility of direct action by rank-and-file members. More of the union's activity is now carried on by lawyers and other experts.

One activity of unions that got a good start during the nineteenth century but that has declined relatively during the twentieth, is to provide an organized social life for their members: the average union probably has a party, picnic, or dance for its members only a few times a year. Only a few unions have made an effort to get spouses and other family members out to union functions. There are seldom union songfests any longer, and probably few members are familiar with union songs. As government and industry have provided social security services, there is less need for the union to stage money-raising events for the benefit of one of the members who is facing a personal or family crisis. The decline of these social affairs may be traced partly to the increasing heterogeneity, both ethnic and residential, of the members of a single local union.

But while these union functions may be declining, there are now more unions, and they serve a larger proportion of the working force. Consequently, unions are more powerful, and, with the aid of more favorable laws, they accomplish more for their members in the sense that they extract more concessions from the employers. At the same time the demands for the sort of psychological satisfactions that the union can provide have probably increased. These satisfactions are a substitute for the hope of rising out of the working class, with the attendant economic and prestige gains of doing so.

[11] John R. Commons *et al.*, *History of Labour in the United States* (4 vols., New York: Macmillan, 1918–1935), especially Vol. IV, *Labor Movements*, by Selig Perlman and Philip Taft. See also (1) Selig Perlman, *A History of Trade Unionism in the United States* (New York: Macmillan, 1937); (2) Sidney Lens, *Left, Right, and Center: Conflicting Forces in American Labor* (Hinsdale, Ill.: H. Regnery Co., 1949).

The economic pattern has gradually changed so that it has become less possible for a worker to become a businessman. The businessmen already in the field established something of a closed union for themselves in their own quest for security, by pooling their individually owned enterprises into huge corporations; consequently the opportunities for newcomers, except through the channel of business and engineering colleges, are slim. It costs more money to start a business, and there is greater need of educated specialists. At the same time the United States cut off the stream of immigration which had hitherto provided a "group farthest down" and which pushed up into new opportunities those workers who were already Americanized.

There was in consequence a steadily growing felt need for worker organization, but this was held down by physical violence organized by the employers and by use of the threat of firing and blacklisting which was easy in the rapidly expanding labor market. Still, the more skilled, and hence less replaceable, workers did successfully organize in strong craft unions. The dream of economic success and independence remained among workers until the 1930's, however, because attitudes seldom change as rapidly as the situation to which they are intended to conform. The Great Depression struck the American worker (and businessman) with a force that has never been fully appreciated. It revealed to most workers that their hopes of rising out of the working class were outmoded myths.[12] And it provided most Americans with a sense of economic insecurity, from which they have not recovered twenty years later. The latter provided the push behind social security legislation. It also provided the stimulus for large-scale expansion of the union movement.

It is a mistaken view of history to assume that the great increase in membership and strength of the trade unions during the mid-1930's was due primarily to the attitude of

[12] This change of attitude has been reported in several studies. See, for example, Caroline B. Rose, "Morale in a Trade Union," *American Journal of Sociology*, LVI (September 1950), 167–174.

President Roosevelt and the opportunities created by Section 7A of the National Recovery Act and later by the Wagner Act. It is true that the Wagner Act facilitated the expansion of unions by preventing employers from taking repressive measures. And President Roosevelt's statement that if he were a worker, he would join a union, was good propaganda that could be used by labor organizers. But the essential fact is that many workers felt, probably for the first time, an impelling need for an organization that would represent their interests in the manipulation of economic power. They realized that they were too weak individually to get for themselves the security they craved, and they found in the trade union an instrument by which many of their needs could be satisfied. There was also a mass psychology favorable to unions during the 1930's, created by their growing success: many workers simply wanted to get on the bandwagon. But this, too, should not be exaggerated, since movements based on faddism alone soon die.

Some union leaders themselves have never understood fully the popular needs which they satisfy. That does not necessarily make them less successful in their day-to-day functioning, especially during the era of economic prosperity which has prevailed from 1938 to the present (1950). But even the most self-centered and dictatorial union leaders are aware that a basic solidarity of their members with the union and a large measure of satisfaction of the members' psychological needs through the union are essential for their successful operation over any significant period of time.[13] They

[13] Some writers — including even some not employer-oriented — fail to perceive this ultimately democratic characteristic of practically all unions in a pluralistic, democratic society. Will Herberg ("Bureaucracy and Democracy in Labor Unions," *Antioch Review*, III [Fall 1943], 405–424), for example, assumes that because member participation is low and because many or most members say, "Let the officials run the union, that's what they're getting paid for," that unions are inevitably and thoroughly undemocratic. It can be maintained, on the contrary, that participation for its own sake — without control and without attitudes that engender and bolster participation — is undemocratic even when it creates the appearance of democracy. The Nazis in Germany in Hitler's day and the Communists in the U.S.S.R. today encourage a great deal of the control-less

learn this especially well when they try to direct their unions into new channels of activity. But aside from this general appreciation of the need for solidarity, many of them have little specific knowledge of the nature of union solidarity. In times of crisis this may be a most dangerous weakness for the union movement.

Businessmen and political leaders too are encrusted with the ideas about workers that were only partially appropriate even in predepression days. Regularly they make mistakes based upon their outmoded assumptions – sometimes with serious consequences for their own interests. (Observe their long adherence to the fallacious assumption that the offer of higher wages alone will make a worker produce more.) Only a realistic understanding of the attitudes and motivations of as large and powerful a section of the American population as the working class can correct their behavior.

It is in such a setting of American history and American attitudes that we present our case study. But the setting does not fully describe contemporary facts. At the beginning of this section we summarized the premises on which the union movement was built. In the body of this report we shall see to what extent the premises conform to existing social facts in the case of one local union.

B. The Locale of the Study

The particular union we have chosen to study is located in the city of St. Louis, Missouri. St. Louis is not a typical city, not only because no existing social phenomenon precisely conforms to an abstract type, but also because it has

but controlled participation precisely because it "harmlessly" works off spontaneous impulses to democracy. The most dictatorial labor leader who permits no "participation" is more democratic than Hitler and Stalin, who encourage "participation," simply because the labor leader is ultimately controlled by the attitudes of even minor groups in his union, if those attitudes are felt strongly enough.

This discussion is not to be considered an argument against participation – as Chapter III will indicate – but rather an argument against the belief that a large amount of participation is an essential and distinguishing characteristic of true democracy.

several unique features that are important influences on its institutions and people. Any conclusion from a study of our union must therefore be qualified before it is generalized to other unions. A brief summary of some of the significant ways in which St. Louis differs from other cities will aid in making such qualifications.

St. Louis is not very far from the geographic center of the United States, and that puts it on the crossroads between East and West, North and South. It has some of the characteristics of all these sections, and some unique characteristics all its own. It has a history as an important commercial city, since it is located on the Mississippi River not far from where the Missouri and Illinois rivers flow into the "father of waters." Today 33 per cent[14] of its people are engaged in manufacturing. Yet none of the factories is very large, and no single industry dominates the scene as in Detroit, Pittsburgh, or even Chicago.[15] The diversification of industry has kept St. Louis from being too hard hit by depressions. This has also meant that St. Louis has been less influenced by the social movements that have followed in the wake of depressions. Particularly relevant is the fact that there are only about 150,000 union members[16] in this city of 850,000 (with a metropolitan area of about 1,250,000 exclusive of some 250,000 in East St. Louis and other towns just across the river in Illinois). Only about 45,000 of the union members are in the CIO, and most of the rest are affiliated with the AF of L.

St. Louis is the oldest large city in the United States west of the Alleghenies. In 1870 it ranked third in population

[14] U.S. Bureau of the Census, *Sixteenth Census of the United States: 1940 Population*, Vol. III, Pt. 3, pp. 924, 926.

[15] That diversity was the major characteristic of manufacturing in the St. Louis Metropolitan Area is demonstrated by the facts that no single industry employed more than 8 per cent of the workers in manufacturing and that the seven leading industries together accounted for less than one third of the manufacturing wage earners in the area. (*Ibid.*)

[16] Estimate based on information given by the St. Louis Industrial Union Council (CIO) and the St. Louis Central Trades and Labor Council (AF of L) in personal interviews, January 1949.

among cities of the United States, being outranked only by New York and Philadelphia. Chicago was then much smaller, and Detroit was a mere town. The relative rate of growth of St. Louis slowed down after that time as the business interests were largely successful in keeping out the giant industries. They first prevented St. Louis from becoming the railroad center of the country by refusing to allow, for some time, the erection of railroad bridges and terminal facilities in the city. At subsequent times the rising meat-packing industry and the infant automobile industry looked favorably on the geographic location of St. Louis, but were discouraged by the obstacles placed in their path by the established business and financial leaders. Even today St. Louis is making no effort to build the kind of airport that cross-continental airlines need in the center of the country. Thus the city has grown relatively slowly,[17] has minimized "outside interference," has avoided much absentee ownership, and continues to look to its indigenous capitalist class for leadership. It is one of the most surprisingly conservative communities in the United States, considering its size.

Since the number of new economic opportunities was kept low, not too many of the "new" immigrants came to St. Louis. St. Louis today has next to the lowest proportion of foreign-born population among the ten largest cities of the United States. Thus the city is "stable" in another sense, and has largely avoided another of the major disturbing influences that America has known. Furthermore, the older immigrants never completely amalgamated into the general life of the city. This is because St. Louis is cut up into relatively isolated neighborhoods by a transportation system that radiates out from the downtown district but has few cross-lines and by an institution called the "private place" – several blocks of houses surrounded by fences and gates and without any through streets. Some of the local neighborhoods of St. Louis are made up of third- and fourth-generation Americans whose

[17] By 1940 it had dropped to eighth place in population rank among American cities.

parents, grandparents, and great-grandparents have lived in those same neighborhoods. Needless to say, these neighborhoods maintain a rural-like intimacy that is also conducive to social conservatism.

Two of the three St. Louis newspapers may be classed as liberal, and they make a great effort to channel national and international news to their readers. There are local affiliates of several liberal national organizations, like the Civil Liberties Committee, the Consumers' Federation, and the National Association for the Advancement of Colored People, but they draw few people into their activities. The same people, totaling a few hundred at the outside, will be the only ones seen in all the civil and social welfare organizations. There is widespread complaint that the rest of the people cannot be drawn out and that St. Louis never gets excited about anything.

Cleavages between various elements of the population are quite sharp. The diversification and local ownership of industry have made for a large upper class, which is much more in control of the city than would be the case if the middle class were larger and more active. With the middle class relatively small and weak, the city seems to be sharply divided between rich and poor.

The Catholic church claims a majority of the churchgoers, although most nonchurchgoers have a Protestant background. In this situation the Protestant clergymen feel that they are weaker than the Catholic priesthood, but *should be* stronger. There are frequent evidences of Catholic-Protestant friction, probably more so than in most American cities. And the cleavage which divides the Catholic and Protestant populations is more significant because of the relatively large proportion of Catholics. Jews of the second or third generation tend to live in geographically separated communities more than they do in those other cities where they also form a small proportion of the population, and St. Louis Jews tend to be more synagogue-affiliated.

Negroes form about 14 per cent (120,000) of the city's

population. While there are no restrictions on their voting, they did not swing their weight concertedly in local elections until 1948. Only 3,000 of them are members of the National Association for the Advancement of Colored People. With a few exceptions, there has been little interracial cooperation. Most civic organizations, including the trade unions, practice segregation. In public institutions the segregation pattern is characteristic of the Border States: there is segregation in the public schools and in theaters, restaurants, and hotels, but there is no segregation in streetcars, railroad stations, or public libraries. Only very recently has there been a concerted effort to break down segregation, and, with the aid of some whites, the movement has been successful in the parks and in some colleges and parochial schools. But in general the Negro community can be characterized as passive and isolated.

Needless to say, we have selected only a few of the characteristics of the St. Louis area for description here—the ones most immediately relevant to the problems of our study.

C. History of the Union[18]

The local union which is now the Warehouse and Distribution Workers, Local 688, International Brotherhood of Teamsters, Chauffeurs, Warehousemen and Helpers of America, American Federation of Labor (hereafter called Teamsters Local 688), started as spontaneously as any organization could. The first shops organized themselves independently and only gradually merged to form a city-wide union in the warehouse and distribution field. They organized during the later years of the depression, when unemployment was still rife but when a measure of confidence and security had returned to workers. It was shortly after the National Labor Relations Act (commonly called the Wagner Act) had been passed, and workers had begun to

[18] Our history is brief and subordinate to our major interest in the solidarity attitudes of the members toward the union. A detailed history is that by Harry V. Ball, Jr., "A Case History of a Local Union," unpublished master's thesis, Washington University (St. Louis, Mo.), 1950.

feel freer to engage in organizational activities without so much fear of reprisals from employers. Still, there was a good deal of conflict in setting up the union, and this created a tradition of hesitancy which the union has to this day. Each shop had a somewhat different history of organization, and all we shall do here is to report on the beginnings of the first and largest shop units.

In February 1937 one of the employees at the warehouse of the J. C. Penney Company went to an AF of L union meeting. He came out convinced that his shop should be organized, and succeeded in getting about twenty-five of his co-workers (out of a total working force of about 500) to meet a union organizer for the Steel Workers Organizing Committee. Organizers' time was scarce then, and the organizer left these workers only with union application cards, which they were to try to get all the workers in their shop to sign. After six or seven weeks of organizational effort, ten of the most active unionists were fired by the company. But under the threat of the Wagner Act all except one were rehired. Then the company organized a company union, but by this time the pro-union workers were so numerous that they took over the company union and filed for an election to be conducted by the National Labor Relations Board (NLRB) under the provisions of the Wagner Act. In June 1937 the employees decided in favor of a CIO union by a margin of 124 votes. The company signed a contract, but shortly thereafter it laid off almost half of its working force – all union members – in an effort to break the union. The remaining workers remained loyal to the union, and during the following nine months the company was forced to hire back the discharged members, and the union remained strong thereafter.

Early 1937 found many discontented workers at the combined production plant and warehouse of the Evans' Coffee Company (145 workers). Wages were extremely low, and there were many seasonal layoffs not based on the seniority principle. The workers read of the CIO organization drive in the daily newspapers, and one of them went to the offices of the much publicized United Electrical Workers, where he was given application cards to get filled out. This worker talked to his fellows, passed out leaflets, and called meetings, and soon he and three others were threatened with discharge. But when they claimed that a majority of the workers were pro-union, the company consented to an NLRB election. The pro-union workers won the election and were given a charter as Local 177A of the United Tea, Coffee and Spice Workers, CIO. The worker who had been successful at Evans' then went out and convinced a majority of workers at the Forbes Coffee Company that they should join his union.

When contracts had been signed with these two coffee houses, the union called on the owner of the third coffee company in St. Louis, the H-P Coffee Company (employing about 40 workers). The owner told the union officers that he would never sign a contract with any union and threatened to call the police. He left that day for a vacation in Florida. As the union president left the owner's office, he told one of the workers in the plant what had happened and urged him to get the workers out on strike the next day. Without any warning to the company, the strike began as scheduled. The vice-president of the company wired the president to come home from Florida, and the contract was signed in two days.

The employees at Butler Brothers' warehouse had tried to form a union in 1933 under the protection of Section 7A of the National Recovery Act (NRA). The company immediately organized a company union in opposition to this effort of the workers and hired most of the officers of the workers' union to fill various management positions. The company union, according to workers recently interviewed, did little for the workers. In the summer of 1937 some of the workers became interested in the organizational activity going on at Penney's and got some of the union officers there to talk at a meeting called for all Butler Brothers' employees. The work was carried on quietly, but soon the company got wind of it and tried to reorganize the company union. But the pro-union workers threatened to call a strike, and the company recognized them without an NLRB election (even though it was later acknowledged that the union did not have a majority of the workers). Thus a new Local Independent Union, affiliated nationally with the CIO, was started.

In 1936 a car unloader at the warehouse of the Shapleigh Hardware Company went to the offices of the AF of L in St. Louis in an effort to get help in organizing his fellow workers. The organizers there asked him what his wages were, then informed him that they were sorry but he was not making enough money even to pay dues. He then went to the offices of the new CIO. There he was welcomed, but the only thing that was done for him was to give him a pile of union application cards to get signed as best he could. This he did, but the work went slowly, and it was not until the summer of 1937 that an NLRB election could be called. The union received 51 per cent of the votes cast and was certified as Local Independent Union 543.

And so it went. One warehouse or production plant after another organized itself, with the aid of the NLRB but with little or no help from the AF of L or the CIO. In some shops the effort failed for a long time. For example, the warehousemen at the Rice-Stix dry goods company began to organize themselves in September 1937. They soon secured a majority and collected dues to purchase a charter from the CIO. But the CIO representative disappeared with the money, and the company laid off 187 of its 228 workers. Only those whom the company considered not likely to attempt to organize another union were returned to their jobs. It was not until 1941, when Harold Gibbons had become head of the warehousemen's joint council, that the Rice-Stix workers were unionized.

As the shops organized into independent locals, they came into contact with each other, either in the process of organization or at the city-wide meetings of the CIO (called the St. Louis Industrial Union Council). The warehousemen realized that they had common problems, and late in 1937 they established an informal board of strategy, which they called the Joint Advisory Council. It had no funds at its disposal for years and functioned largely by getting members of its organizing committee to give lectures and pass out leaflets at various unorganized shops.

The St. Louis CIO put pressure on the warehouse locals to affiliate with some international union in the CIO, preferably the United Retail Employees Union. The Joint Advisory Council affiliates realized that they were too weak to remain independent, and although they resisted the idea of joining a union of retail workers rather than of warehousemen, they did join this international in February 1939. The St. Louis Joint Advisory Council sent a large delegation to the 1939 convention of the International in Detroit to demand the establishment of a Wholesale and Warehouse Division within the International. The convention endorsed this program, and also changed the name of the International. With further changes it became the United Retail, Wholesale, and Department Store Employees of America (URWDSEA, CIO). However, because of International President Samuel Wolchok's opposition, the warehouse division did not begin to function until 1941.

Since union dues of the International were lower than they had been for the St. Louis groups as local independent unions, some of the difference was contributed to the Joint Advisory Council for organizational purposes. This little treasury, as well as the funds of all the locals connected with the Joint Advisory Council, was soon spent in a strike which secured the union shop for the Shapleigh Hardware workers. However, organizational work did proceed and a few more small shops joined the Joint Advisory Council, although one of the large original unions at the Blackwell-Wielandy Company was broken by a strike.

There was increasing friction between the St. Louis Joint

Advisory Council and the international URWDSEA because President Wolchok had refused to set up the new Wholesale and Warehouse Division, had not kept his promise to return some of the increased dues to the locals for organizational work, and had tried to get the St. Louis locals to amalgamate instead of remaining loosely affiliated with each other through the Joint Advisory Council. In May 1941 Wolchok sent Harold J. Gibbons to the Joint Advisory Council to take charge of it, without consulting the St. Louis locals. The local leaders resented the intruder for some time, but Gibbons won them over by his militant organizational policy and by his sending local leaders to summer workers' education schools.

Shortly after Gibbons came, workers at Rice-Stix, Handling, Inc., and Witte Hardware Company were brought into the union; there were two successful strikes; and there was a closer integration of the locals making up the Joint Advisory Council (including a change of its name to Joint Council). All the warehouses (except Shapleigh's) merged into Local 11 and formed a single unit in the Joint Council. Other units in the council were, then, Shapleigh's, the Coffee House Local 177A, the National Candy Local 310, and the small department store Local 372. By early 1943, when the Mavrakos Candy Company workers were brought into the union, the Joint Council under Gibbons claimed 4,100 members. The shops organized up to that time are the ones studied in the survey reported on in the succeeding chapters of this book.

During the war, the union ran into difficulties because of the Federal government's policy against wage raises and because of the failure of its drive to organize department store workers. The department store campaign involved the union in a long-drawn-out fight before the NLRB and in a lawsuit that was carried up to the Supreme Court of the United States. The union compensated for failure to get wage increases by setting up the Labor Health Institute (LHI), whereby the employers paid for a full program of medical care for most of the workers and their families, and by getting sick leave and vacation clauses into contracts.[19] It partially compensated for failure in the department store field by organizing workers in small food production shops.

Gibbons was convinced of the importance of workers' education, and in addition to sending a few shop stewards every summer to the workers' school at the University of Wisconsin, he set up a newspaper, the *Midwest Labor World* (in 1943), as a means of keeping the membership constantly oriented regarding union problems and union policy. The newspaper also carries news of labor outside the union and seeks to promote a liberal policy in race relations, politics, and other matters outside the narrow sphere of strict trade unionism. During the war, also, and despite his major defeat in the department store drive, Gibbons was one of the CIO leaders actively planning for a third political party.

Because of his militancy and his successes, Gibbons emerged from the war period a highly popular and respected leader of the union. When the war restrictions against wage increases were relaxed and the cost of living jumped upward as a consequence of President Truman's removal of rationing controls and Congress's removal of price controls, the union entered a new period of militant effort to get wage increases and other worker benefits. In this campaign it was more often successful than not.

Resistance against amalgamation within the unions was somewhat reduced, and a food and candy local (Local 7) was formed out of the hitherto independent locals at the National Candy Company (Local 310), the coffee houses (Local 177A), the newly organized food shops, and some of the older food shops that had previously joined with the warehouse shops in Local 11. This occurred in 1945, and also in the same year the Negro taxicab drivers of St. Louis were brought into the Joint Council as Local 22. They did not logically belong in this union, but no other union wanted

[19] In 1949 about 60 per cent of the members were covered by LHI and by sick leave clauses, according to a speech made by Harold Gibbons at Kiel Auditorium in St. Louis on August 9, 1949.

them, largely because they were Negroes. Gibbons' no-discrimination policy was well known, and fairly rare in St. Louis.[20] In 1947 a new local (Local 464) of workers in small clothing stores was brought into the Joint Council, which changed its name to St. Louis Joint Board about this time. In 1947 the union had about 6,000 members, engaged in a wide variety of occupations and industries and organized into four superficially autonomous locals affiliated with the Joint Board, whose salaried director was Harold J. Gibbons.

As indicated previously, the union had always been somewhat uneasy about its relationship with its International, URWDSEA. The International, headed by Samuel Wolchok, in its turn regarded the St. Louis local as too independent, too militant, and troublesome. Wolchok had sent Gibbons to St. Louis to control the Joint Council for him, but Gibbons came to express the attitudes of the local leaders better than they were able to themselves. Gibbons provided sophistication, technique, and increased direction to a union that already had democracy and militancy. Thus the underlying friction remained between the St. Louis organization and its international foster parent. Locals in a few other cities affiliated with URWDSEA also felt something of the same hostility. They felt that URWDSEA was not aggressive enough in organization, too domineering in its relations with its locals, and even that it might be corrupt.

A crisis developed in 1944 when Wolchok failed to win the Montgomery Ward strike in Chicago, despite huge expenditures of funds. There were charges that he had misused the funds, that he had not followed the mandates of the International conventions, and that he was working with the

[20] In December 1945 Gibbons received the CIO award for carrying out the no-discrimination policy. Among the activities for which the union received this award were: (1) Engaging in interracial sports in St. Louis' largest public park, thereby establishing a precedent which led to general use of the park's sports' facilities by Negroes. (2) Holding interracial banquets and balls in some St. Louis hotels, leading to a no-discrimination policy in at least one of them. (3) Employing Negro office girls. (4) Putting no-discrimination clauses into contracts with employers. (5) Standing firm against wildcat strikes called to protest the upgrading of Negroes.

Communists in their policy of avoiding all action that might weaken the war effort. Gibbons was one of the accusers, and along with others he demanded a thorough investigation of the International's policies and practices. Wolchok reciprocated allegedly by sending a spy to St. Louis, ostensibly to work as an organizer for Gibbons but actually to try to bribe some of the rank-and-file leaders in St. Louis to work against Gibbons, and finally by putting Gibbons and his fellow rebels on trial before the International's executive committee. The rebels unsuccessfully appealed to Philip Murray, as head of the CIO, to condemn Wolchok as corrupt and ineffective.[21] They were read out of URWDSEA, but their local memberships supported them to the extent of breaking off the affiliation with the International.

Thus it came about, in January 1948, that the St. Louis Joint Board of URWDSEA became the independent local known as the United Distribution Workers (UDW), affiliated with the CIO through the St. Louis Industrial Union Council but not affiliated with any international union. In making the break, the local leaders fully realized that they would have to join some other international, because an independent local, especially one servicing such a wide range of industries, is weak. Gibbons and other local leaders canvassed the possibilities throughout 1948, and at the beginning of February 1949 effected a merger with Local 688 of the International Brotherhood of Teamsters, AF of L.[22] The old Teamsters Local added about 2,000 members to the

[21] In December 1948, a year after some of the important locals had broken away from URWDSEA, Murray strongly criticized Wolchok for failure to organize effectively. He took the department store jurisdiction away from URWDSEA and transferred it to the Amalgamated Clothing Workers, CIO. The rebuke was so strong that Wolchok was removed from the presidency of URWDSEA, and the much weakened International reorganized to maintain itself in the retail and wholesale shops it still retained.

[22] The old Teamsters Local 688 – like the more recently organized shops in the St. Louis Joint Board – was organized from the top rather than by the rank and file, as was the case with most of the shops studied in our survey. It differed from the St. Louis Joint Board also in not encouraging membership participation in union decisions and in avoiding "fringe issues" – that is, those union activities outside of strict wages-hours control.

union (which had become fully amalgamated upon breaking with URWDSEA), and after another short organizing campaign, the new Teamsters Local 688 had about 8,500 members. More important, the merger brought the local into one of the most powerful and aggressive international unions in the country, the Teamsters.

This shift evoked in CIO circles much criticism of Gibbons as a deserter. Despite these antagonisms on the part of other St. Louis union leaders, the union, now Teamsters Local 688, seemed to have reached new heights of power and to be headed upward. The first major development, beginning in March 1949, was a concerted drive, with two other St. Louis AF of L unions, to organize the department store workers. This was the situation in which the union found itself at the time of our survey.[23]

[23] Shortly after the field work on the survey was completed, the union leadership ran into a series of difficulties: (1) On orders from Dave Beck, International vice-president, Gibbons broke with the other two unions in the department store drive and started an unsuccessful raid on the organized shops of one of them (the Retail Clerks union). (2) The technique of organizing department store salespeople by talking to them while purchasing something was discouraged by a federal judge's *obiter dictum* that he would probably judge this practice illegal if the issue were before him, since organization was being done on company time and company property. (3) These two events broke the department store drive. (4) The year-old Grady strike, on which a great deal of money had been spent, was broken by an unfavorable decision by the NLRB. (5) An issue arose in the union staff over the question of opposing the licensing of more cab drivers by the city council. (6) Many members expressed opposition to further contributions for new organization in view of the department store failure and argued that new assessments be tied up for a strike fund. Despite these many difficulties occurring at one time, which depleted the union's treasury at a time of economic recession and which raised questions about the competence of some of the union's leaders, the union's morale was strong enough to surmount the crisis and allow the union to grow and have continued successes.

CHAPTER II

How the Study Was Done

The group studied in this survey constitutes a representative sample of those members of Local 688 whose shops were organized into the union before 1943. That is, the shops studied are the large core around which the union has expanded and expects to expand further in the future. Workers in these shops constituted 72 per cent of the total membership of the union in the winter of 1948–1949, before the amalgamation with the Teamsters and before the organization drive in the spring of 1949. In the summer of 1949 these "old" shops still constituted 51 per cent of the total estimated membership of the union. There is little doubt that the attitudes of the members of these shops would be different from those of the original Teamsters and from those of the newly organized shops. The study is limited, then, to the members of the union whose shops have been organized into this union for at least seven years.

While the shops studied had been in the union at least since 1943, that does not mean, of course, that all the members studied had been in the union for that length of time. The shops have experienced the usual turnover of members which would be typical of unions in this field of economic endeavor. About three fifths of the union members included in the representative sample studied cannot date their membership back as long as seven years. The study should not be thought of as one of "old union members," then, but rather

TABLE 1. DISTRIBUTION OF UNION MEMBERS BY SHOP AND COMPOSITION OF THE SAMPLE STUDIED *

Shop	Industry	Number of Union Members Employed	Percentage from Shop of Total Union Membership	Percentage from Shop of Total Completed Schedules
Shapleigh Hardware	Wholesale hardware ..	922	21.4	20.9
Rice-Stix	Wholesale dry goods ..	584	13.5	14.2
Chase Candy	Manufacturing and wholesale candy ..	571	13.2	12.5
Brown Shoe	Wholesale shoes (some manufacturing)	467	10.8	10.2
J. C. Penney	Wholesale dry goods ...	393	9.1	10.2
Handling	Wholesale dry goods ...	284	6.6	6.9
Butler Brothers	Wholesale general merchandise ...	254	5.9	5.4
Union Biscuit	Manufacturing and wholesale crackers.	232	5.4	5.8
Mavrakos	Manufacturing and wholesale candy ..	137	3.2	2.3
Switzer Candy	Manufacturing and wholesale candy ..	136	3.1	3.6
Witte Hardware	Wholesale hardware ..	91	2.1	1.8
Forbes Coffee	Manufacturing and wholesale coffee ..	90	2.1	1.8
A. S. Aloe	Wholesale surgical supplies	87	2.0	2.6
Old Judge (Evans) Coffee	Manufacturing and wholesale coffee ..	52	1.2	1.0
H. P. Coffee	Manufacturing and wholesale coffee ..	16	0.4	0.8
Total		4,316	100.0	100.0

* Only shops that had been organized for at least seven years are included.

of members of shops that have a history of at least seven years' stable organization.

The predominant industry represented by the union membership studied is wholesale trade and warehouse work. All of the companies for whom the members worked were at least partly in this industry, although a few have a greater proportion of their workers manufacturing the items which they then proceed to sell wholesale. Table 1 lists the names of the companies employing the workers studied, with an indication of the industry and of the number of workers employed at the time the sample was drawn (February 1949). As may be inferred from Table 1, a majority (50.6 per cent) of the workers had jobs as packers, order-fillers, etc. Almost 20 per cent had manufacturing jobs. Some 15 per cent were in clerical occupations, and the remainder were in such miscellaneous occupations as custodial and service work, machine repair, and truck driving.

The sample of workers chosen for study was strictly representative. The union has an alphabetical card file of all its members, separated according to the company they work for. The sampling procedure was simply to take the name and address from every 9th card from those companies to be sampled, omitting only the small proportion who live across the river in Illinois. The number 9 was chosen as the one most likely to provide a sample large enough for the analysis deemed necessary and small enough to be reached with the number of interviewers available. A total of 475 names and addresses were copied in this way from the union files.

Since interviewing was carried on in the workers' homes, it was expected that there would be a large loss from the sample originally secured. The loss was not so large as originally expected: 392 interviews were completed out of the 475 in the original sample. Further, many of the losses were of a sort that were not likely to represent distorting bias in the results. Table 2 lists the reasons why the 83 cases in the original sample were not secured. A study of the table suggests that only the 19 persons who refused to be interviewed

TABLE 2. REASONS FOR THE "LOSS" OF 83 CASES FROM THE SAMPLE

Reason	Number of Cases	Probable Bias Involved
Were fired or left the job	23	Insignificant bias: low seniority or poor work; women leaving for housework
Refused to be interviewed (2 said they didn't know anything about the union, 5 said they didn't want to be bothered, 1 said union shop steward had told her not to talk to anyone, 11 gave no reason)	19	Bias created in the sample by most of these, but direction of bias unknown
Moved and address untraceable	11	Probably no bias, or slight mobility bias
Withdrawn from sample because lived too far out in the country for convenient contact	9	Insignificant bias
Not at home after 3 or more visits	7	Possible minor mobility bias
Ill in bed or in the hospital for weeks	6	Possible minor age bias
On vacation for several weeks while interviewing was being completed	5	Probably no bias
Judged by interviewer to be of too low intelligence to follow through on interview	2	Minor intelligence bias
Said he had already been interviewed, but no record	1	Probably no bias

are likely to constitute a significant bias in the sample. These 19 cases constitute 4 per cent of the total original sample—a proportion not large enough to distort the findings seriously. Further, it is not likely that all 19 cases form a bias in the same direction—at least 1 of the 19 indicated by her reason for refusal to be interviewed that she was pro-union; perhaps most of the others were anti-union since there was union sanction for the survey.[1] However, refusal to be interviewed, coupled with differential firing and voluntary leaving of the job among the different companies studied, has

[1] Union sanction was not complete, however, since a refusal came from a member who had asked her shop steward about the survey. According to the member, the steward said it was not necessary to answer as the survey had only a political motive.

hardly any effect on the distribution of those interviewed for the study: The last two columns of Table 1 show that the distribution of those whose interviews were completed is approximately the same as the total number of employees in the companies studied. In view of all the facts, we feel justified in considering the 392 cases analyzed in this report to be a representative sample of the selected shops. We shall therefore generalize our findings from the sample studied to the older shops of the union as a whole.

Interviews were carried on by the author and his students at Washington University. Since some of the interviewers were volunteers, some of them secured as few as one interview apiece. No single interviewer secured more than twenty interviews. Each interviewer had a minimum of two hours' training in groups, and some interviewers had more training. Interviewer training was in terms of both general approach and ways of handling specific questions. A minority of the interviewers had previous experience in interviewing. Immediate checks were made on returned schedules, and faults were noted. In two cases the interviewers did so poorly that they were tactfully withdrawn from the work.

The questions for the schedule were prepared with suggestions from union officials as well as from trained social scientists. The advice of the former was heeded with respect to the subject matter of the questions in many cases, but not with respect to the form of the questions. Some of the questions—among those dealing with attitudes toward Negroes and Jews—were taken from previous studies.[2] The questions were pretested for reliability (understandability and unambiguity) and validity (relevance to the issue up for study) on small groups of union members, and two major revisions in the entire schedule were made. When the survey was completed, it was not felt that all the questions secured the exact

[2] The author wishes to acknowledge his borrowing of questions from studies by Dr. Paul Lazarsfeld, the Department of Scientific Research of the American Jewish Committee, and the Citizens Council on Housing and Community Planning of St. Louis.

sort of information which the investigator and sponsors of the study originally desired. But satisfaction with the schedule was very high. The weaknesses in the schedule will be indicated in the body of the report and in Appendix 1.

The general approach to the interview was twofold: (1) The study was sponsored by the union and was in the interests of all union members. (2) The interviewer and the study director were scientists or students who had no direct connection with the union and were solely interested in frank, complete, and anonymous answers to the questions. These two threads will be seen running throughout the following descriptions of the procedure in making appointments and conducting interviews.

The first contact the average union member had with the survey was by reading about it in the union's newspaper, which reaches about 80 per cent of the membership. The first story, a regular news report by the editor, appeared on the lower part of the front page of the February 23, 1949, issue of *Midwest Labor World*:

WASHINGTON UNIVERSITY OFFER TO SURVEY ATTITUDES OF UNION MEMBERS ACCEPTED BY STEWARDS

Washington University's offer to make a survey of the attitudes of members toward the Union was accepted by the Stewards Council in a majority vote Tuesday, after extended discussion.

The survey will be made by trained interviewers under guidance of the Washington sociology department. President Harold J. Gibbons urged the stewards to take advantage of the offer.

The survey will work this way:

Interviewers will be given access to Union records to select at random the names and addresses of a cross-section of the membership.

The interviewers will contact these members, and ask a number of questions on how they feel about the Union's policies and the way the Union operates.

The information secured by the interviewers will be confidential.

The report back to the Union will be in terms of percentages –

a certain percentage believes the Union is democratic enough, a certain percentage believes the Union could be more democratic, a certain percentage believes it is too democratic, etc. Such matters as union dues, fines, assessments, strike policies, race policy would be included in the survey.

Supporting the proposal Gibbons said that he, the staff and the stewards had sometimes failed to foresee what the membership thought.

"I want to have the information that will enable us to improve our Union when it can be done on good trade union lines," he said. "I want to know where we must concentrate education when a section of the membership shows poor trade union attitudes. I want information that will tell me whether wholehearted support or not can be obtained on a policy recommendation I make. Possibly this survey will be only 80% accurate, but discounting errors, I think it can be very valuable to our Union."[3]

A month later, during the week in which field work began, the union newspaper contained the following story concerning the survey in a key spot on the upper part of the front page:

INTERVIEW SURVEY IS STARTED

Some union members were surprised the last few days by getting phone calls or postcards asking them to make appointments to be interviewed by students from Washington University. This is part of the study by Teamsters Local 688 to learn what the members think about the Union and what they want the Union to do in the future. It's one way for rank-and-filers to get their ideas over to Pres. Harold J. Gibbons and to the chief shop stewards and the union staff.

Of course, not everyone in our big Union can be interviewed. The idea is to get some members from each of the shops that have been in the Union for some time. Persons to be interviewed were selected from an alphabetical list of members, taking every 9th name. So if you are one of those who gets an interview, you know your name was picked by chance.

Teachers and students from Washington University are doing the interviewing. We thought you might like it better talking to

[3] *Midwest Labor World* (St. Louis, Mo.), February 23, 1949, p. 1.

an outsider, especially a young man or woman who is interested in what you have to say.

The interview will be in your own home, at a time that you agree on with the student. He or she will have the questions printed up ahead of time, and will read them off to you. We at the Union office have put into these questions just about everything we can think of right now. We hope you'll find them interesting and get a kick out of them.

Please answer frankly! Don't hesitate to speak out and say what you really think. Your answers will be added up with answers from other members before they are reported back to us. In this way we will know what all the members interviewed are saying, but we won't know what your personal answers are. Your personal answers will be completely confidential, and your name will not be put on what you say. The idea is to give you a chance to speak freely and yet with a good purpose.

There are no right or wrong answers to the questions. It's what you think that counts. This will be a chance for a lot of you to get your ideas over.

Help the students a little. Some are interviewing for the first time, and some are scared. Make them feel at home. Each student will carry a letter from Gibbons so you can know that it's o.k. for him to interview you. Please answer all the questions, so we can get all points of view. The interview will take only about an hour.

Have fun! [4]

Each interviewer carried a copy of this issue of the union's newspaper in case the respondent had not seen it and was doubtful as to the sponsorship of the survey. In addition, each interviewer carried an introductory letter, on union stationery, signed by the union's director, and with the interviewer's name written in on the blank provided. This letter read as follows:

Dear Fellow Member:

Your union wants to do the best for all its members. As you know, we've already done a lot—like getting higher wages, set-

[4] *Ibid.*, March 23, 1949, p. 1.

ting up the Labor Health Institute, putting out our own newspaper, and so on. But we're not completely sure what you think about each and every one of these things. Also, we've got to make some plans for the future, and your ideas are needed before we can even start discussing future plans in union meetings and voting on them. In a democratic union, every member gets a chance to say what he thinks about everything affecting the union.

So we're asking you to answer some important questions about the union. Some teachers and students from Washington University are working with us, and we'd like to introduce ________ who comes with this letter to interview you. Don't hesitate to speak out and say what you really think. Your answers will be added up with answers from other members before they are reported to me and to the shop stewards. In this way we will know what all the members interviewed are saying, but we won't know what your personal answers are. Your personal answers will be completely confidential.

So please give a little time and thought to the questions the interviewer will ask you.

Yours, for the best possible Union,
[SIGNED]
Harold J. Gibbons, *President*
Local 688

When the field work was well under way, on April 13, 1949, the newspaper printed the following shorter article on the lower part of its front page:

UNION SURVEY IN FULL SWING

The students from Washington University who are interviewing on the union membership survey are all busy these days. Some are making appointments by telephone or postcard, but most are just coming right up to the homes of union members. Names and addresses are taken off the union files on a purely chance basis, so whether you get chosen or not has nothing to do with you personally.

But in order to get a good survey, everyone chosen must cooperate by answering the questions. The students report that only a few are refusing. Then we send them right back again. The idea is to get every kind of union member in the survey: Old and young, those who come to meetings and those who don't, those who like the union and those who don't. Every kind of person must be given a chance to say what he thinks. If you are interviewed you are not only talking for yourself, but for others who think and feel like you do.

Help the student a little. Some are interviewing for the first time, and some are scared. Make them feel at home. We think you'll enjoy the interview, and you may be helping the whole union.[5]

When the survey began, it was hoped that most appointments for interviews could be made by telephone or by double government postcard (that is, one card stating the purpose of the desired appointment and the return card providing space for the respondent to indicate the time at which he could keep an appointment at his home). The postcard proved to be almost completely ineffective, despite the fact that it was represented as sent out by the union's director. The telephone approach to an appointment served effectively with about 70 per cent of those union members who could be reached in this way. But correct telephone numbers were available for less than half of the sample. Most did not have telephones listed in their names, and the union had no record of home telephone numbers. For this reason most interviews were conducted either without prior appointment or by appointments made at the door of the workers' homes. In 5 cases appointments were made for the interview by a shop steward, and in 14 other cases (in one shop) interviews were conducted at the union meeting place after a union meeting.

Instructions to interviewers regarding the making of appointments were provided on a mimeographed sheet. Later the modification was made that the interviewer should pro-

[5] *Ibid.*, April 13, 1949, p. 1. The four documents quoted in full above represent the official connection the survey had with the union, from the standpoint of the average worker.

ceed directly with a home visit if no telephone was available or if he had been refused, for any reason whatsoever, an appointment by telephone. These instructions and an introduction to the interview were taught and explained to the interviewers. They read as follows:

MAKING APPOINTMENTS

1*a*. You will be given a list of names and addresses of persons whom you are to interview. In some cases, a telephone number, too. It is best to make appointments over the telephone, so if you don't have a number given, look it up in the telephone book. If you have a home phone number, a good time to call is 5:00 to 6:30 p.m. If you have to call the place of employment, ask the company operator to have the respondent call you back, at your number, and at such and such a time.

b. If you can't use the telephone, use a double post card, which the respondent can send back to indicate what time he can see you. Post cards will be furnished you for this purpose. You will have to put on the respondent's address, the return address (the interviewer's address), and any limitations regarding time of appointment. Also put the respondent's code number on the bottom of the return card.

c. If neither telephone nor post card reaches the respondent, you should go to his house directly. Many people are shy or scared, and you have to follow them up. A good time to arrive is 6:00 p.m. Remember that most working people are through work at 4:00 p.m.; they eat at 5:00 p.m., and may want to leave the house at 7:00 p.m. Since most of the respondents assigned to you live in the same area, you can go to one of these houses on the same evening as you have an appointment with another respondent. While you shouldn't make two appointments in one evening, unless they are two hours apart, you should never make a trip to see one respondent without tackling another for whom you have no appointment.

d. If none of these methods works, see a chief interviewer or Dr. Rose.

2. When arriving for an appointment (never be late; always early), ask to speak to Mr. or Mrs. ______ ______ (the person with whom you have an appointment). If that person is not in,

ask if he will be in in a few minutes. If not, say that you are the interviewer for the union, and that you had an appointment with Mr. ______ ______ for this evening, and do you (the person answering the door) know anything about it. Perhaps the answerer can make an appointment for another day. If not, ask the answerer to please take a message to the respondent. Write it down on a sheet of paper, saying, "I came at ______ o'clock for our appointment, but you weren't at home. Would you please 'phone me at ______ to set another time when I can see you? I am usually home around ______ o'clock. (Your signature.)"

3. To make an appointment by telephone: After you are sure you are speaking to the right person, say: "I don't think you know me, but my name is ______ ______. Mr. Harold Gibbons, the director of your union, has asked me to get in touch with some members of the union in order to ask them some questions. You happen to be one of those picked for this interview. I was wondering when I might come to your home and talk to you for about an hour."

If the respondent says he has no time, or doesn't want to be interviewed, say: "This is for your good. It's one of the ways Mr. Gibbons can find out what's on your mind, when he doesn't have as much time as he would like to get in touch with you personally. Also, you should know that we don't put your name down on what you say. The idea is to find out what union members generally are thinking, not to put you personally on the spot."

If the respondent asks why you picked him, say: "We are getting some from every shop. You were picked by chance from the whole list of people in your shop." If he asks why don't you ask somebody else, say: "We want to talk to all kinds of union members, those who like the union and those who don't; those who know a lot about it and those who don't. So you see, we can't let anybody say "no" because we want to find out what every kind of person is thinking. Won't you please let me come out to your house and see you for a while?"

If the respondent doesn't want to make an appointment, argue politely and in a friendly way with him for a while, using the above arguments. You can read the letter from Gibbons over the 'phone. If the respondent still refuses finally, say: "Well, I'm very sorry you won't help out. Do I have to give you up as hopeless? ————. Well, then, I'm sorry. Goodbye."

Check the respondent's address before hanging up, after having made the appointment.

Report immediately to a chief interviewer the name of any person who refuses to see you.

INTRODUCTION TO INTERVIEW

(First be sure you are talking to the person you came to see.)

I'm John Jones, a student at Washington University. You remember that I called you up about seeing you to ask you some questions about your union. The union wants to find out what you think of some of the things it has been doing, and I'm here to ask the questions.

Now we can't interview everybody in your big union, so we're meeting with some from every shop. You were just picked by chance; no special reason why you were picked rather than some other worker in your shop. So we're not interested in you personally right now, and your name will *not* be attached to anything you say. We only want to know what the members of this union generally are thinking, and so I'll scratch your name off of the answer sheet.

This is your chance to say what you think about the union, and let the director and the staff know what's on your mind — what you like, and what you don't like. What you say might help your union do a better job for you. Say what you really think, not what you think someone else would like you to say.

(If you haven't been invited to come in and sit down by this time, ask if you might come in so the two of you can be comfortable while you talk. If the respondent is suspicious, and doesn't want to cooperate, show him the letter from Gibbons, saying: "Here is a letter from Mr. Harold Gibbons, the director of your union, saying that it's o.k. for you to talk to me about the union.")

Now I'm going to ask these questions, and please answer them the way you think best. There are no right or wrong answers; it's what you think that counts. Sometimes possible answers are given here, which I'll read to you, and all you have to do then is to tell me which answer is the best one. Here is the first question:

Remember:

1. Be friendly to the respondent as a *person*, but never agree or disagree with what he is saying. Don't show your attitude on union matters *at all.* If the respondent asks what you think, say that these questions are for the union members only to answer, and that you don't know enough about the union to answer.

2. Read each question and the list of answers *completely*, without changing a single word. If the respondent doesn't seem to understand, read the question, without the answer, alone, once more and slowly. If he still doesn't understand, try changing a few words, but keep the meaning. Put a circle around the number of the question for which you had to change the words on the third try.

3. Always be polite. The easiest way to overcome the respondent's anger or discourtesy is to be cool, firm, and polite yourself. Don't swear even if the respondent does. If you wish to smoke, ask the respondent's permission.

4. Don't talk about yourself, except to say that you are a student at Washington University. Remember that the best interviewer is always something of a stranger – objective and aloof, even though friendly and human.

5. Don't let the respondent get off the subject. Tell him politely but firmly that the question wants to know ________. If he starts to get too lengthy in his answer, even though it is relevant, say: "I think you've given a good answer to that question; now the next question is: ________." Write his extra comments, if relevant, briefly next to the checked answer.

6. If wife or someone else is present, be sure you get the respondent's opinion, and not the other person's.

7. On the "free" answer, you may have to condense a little – just as in taking notes at a lecture. But don't put words in the respondent's mouth. If you think your interpretation is important, write it down but put brackets around it.

8. If you have difficulty with the first or second interview, consult one of the chief interviewers. If one of the questions gives you trouble several times, consult one of the chief interviewers. If you can't reach a chief interviewer, call Dr. Rose at Parkview 4700, Station 380.

9. Women interviewers can take a friend along if they prefer.

Remember that the respondents are steady, honest working people, who have worked in the same company for several years, and you are in no danger from them. If they are uncordial, it is either because they have personal problems or because they are suspicious or frightened of you.

One of the greatest difficulties in reaching the union members was a result of their high mobility (despite the housing shortage!). The union's list of addresses was out of date by as much as a year. Approximately 20 per cent of the members were not found at the address which had been listed for them. With the aid of neighbors, union meeting attendance cards, the telephone directory, and in some cases telephone calls to the employers (by a union official), all but eleven of those with old addresses were located or were ascertained to have left the union and the job.

Interviewers made it a practice to call at the members' houses at a time when they were most likely to be at home and available for an interview. The time immediately after supper, a later hour in the evening, Saturday, and Sunday were, in this order, the best times for finding union members at home. Excuses and refusals were not numerous, as we have seen. While the interviewer was instructed to remain formally polite under all circumstances, a first excuse or refusal was never taken as final. Where an excuse was given, the same interviewer would try once more. When a refusal was given, or the second excuse appeared lame, another interviewer was sent (usually of the opposite sex or of a different personality type).

On the whole, there was good response to the interview on the part of the members. Interviewers were asked to rate the cooperativeness of each respondent on a scale of A, B, C, D, F. A majority of 53.8 per cent were given an A rating, another 24.0 per cent got a B rating. Only 12.2 per cent got a C rating, 4.1 per cent a D rating, and 0.8 per cent an F rating (3.6 per cent filled out the questionnaire themselves and so were not rated; another 1.5 per cent were not given a rating). In only two cases did interviews once started fail of completion. One of these was terminated by the interviewer, who felt that the respondent was incapable of understanding the questions. The other was terminated by the respondent's father (in a brusque manner) after the respondent herself had started most cooperatively. Two respondents had such poor command of the English language that the interview had to be conducted through an interpreter. There were several instances of unusual and friendly cooperation: several times the interviewers were invited for dinner or a glass of beer or some other refreshment. Some respondents gave answers in such detail that the interviews took over three hours apiece (the interview could be completed readily in about fifty minutes). In a few cases the interviewer was invited to return for a social engagement.

CHAPTER III

Participation and Loyalty

Solidarity with a group has many facets and is manifested in several ways.[1] In this chapter we shall examine various kinds of participation in union activities and various verbal expressions of loyalty to the union as indexes of solidarity. In subsequent chapters we shall consider the extent to which members agree with union policies and the extent to which there is cleavage between various categories of union members as further indexes of solidarity. In each case there will be an attempt to analyze the social and psychological sources of the manifestation of solidarity or lack of it, although this analysis is far from complete because of limitations of the method of research.

In the present chapter, for example, there is an initial assumption that the members' willingness to participate in union activities is a function of their feelings of solidarity. This assumption is provided at least a partial test by showing

[1] Probably the first theoretical discussion of social solidarity is that of the pioneer sociologist, Émile Durkheim, *Division of Labor in Society* (1st ed., Paris, 1893; latest American ed., Glencoe, Ill.: Free Press, 1947). Studies of solidarity in specific groups have been carried on by social scientists in industry, the armed forces, and ethnic groups. See, for example: (1) F. J. Roethlisberger and W. J. Dickson, *Management and the Worker* (Cambridge, Mass.: Harvard University Press, 1939); (2) S. F. Miyamoto, *Social Solidarity Among the Japanese in Seattle*, University of Washington Publication in the Social Sciences, II, No. 2 (December 1939), 57–130; (3) Samuel A. Stouffer *et al.*, *The American Soldier* (2 vols., Princeton: Princeton University Press, 1949); (4) Arnold M. Rose, *The Negro's Morale: Group Identification and Protest* (Minneapolis: University of Minnesota Press, 1949).

the relation between participation and other manifestations of solidarity. Participation is measured by members' statements specifying their attendance at union meetings, speaking up at these meetings, estimations of interest in union activities, preferences for attending meetings as compared to attending nonunion social functions, supporting negotiating committees during periods of contract negotiation, reading and understanding the contract, and serving on picket lines during times of strike. Verbal expressions of loyalty include statements of need for a union in general, of satisfaction with the way this particular union is run, and of satisfaction with the work and characteristics of the union staff members. Sources of these manifestations of solidarity are sought in the stated desire for democratic control of the union, in the feeling of satisfaction with the accomplishments of the union, in the feeling of opposition to the employer, in reasons for joining the union, in beliefs as to the purposes of the union, and in the psychological support of union membership given by the family of the member. Some of these are shown to be probable bases of solidarity and others not.

Such is the structure of this chapter. We shall now examine the facts.

A. Participation of the Members in the Activities of the Union

Unions vary considerably in the degree to which their members participate in the activities of the union. On the one hand, there are unions in which all decisions are made by the top officials and there is never a meeting of the rank-and-file membership. On the other hand, there are unions in which the rank-and-file membership meets regularly, makes itself felt on every significant issue, and shifts its top leadership when it feels that general policy is wrong.

Teamsters Local 688 tends to have a high level of member participation, although probably not so high as in some unions. The norm is one meeting a month,[2] but legitimate

[2] This norm exists not only as a union rule, but also in the minds of the

excuses and summer vacations would naturally pare that figure down. If we take seven meetings a year as the minimum criterion of conscientious attendance, Table 3 shows

TABLE 3. ATTENDANCE AT UNION MEETINGS

Meetings Attended in the Past Year	Percentage Attending	
	Of Total Membership	Of Members in Union at Least 1 Year
None	7.8	5.7
1–2	9.6	5.5
3–6	30.7	23.6
7–12	41.3	53.2
Over 12	9.1	10.6
"Don't know"; no answer	1.5	1.4
Total	100.0	100.0
Number	392	343

that the majority of members meet this criterion. Considering only those members who have been in the union at least one year (and who therefore have had the opportunity to attend all meetings during the year), 35 per cent are significantly delinquent in attendance (six or fewer meetings attended). However, only 5.7 per cent have not attended any meetings. And 10.6 per cent attend more than the norm, the majority of these being shop stewards who have numerous special meetings.

Until shortly before the study was conducted, union meetings were held on a "crew" basis (25 or fewer workers with a shop steward for each crew). The dominant mode of meeting as this is being written is the "shop" meeting (all workers at one plant, with a shop steward for each 25 workers or smaller remaining fraction and a chief shop steward for the whole plant). Perhaps once a year there is an all-union meeting.

Reasons given for nonattendance at union meetings are revealing. The reasons were given in answer to the open

members. When asked to specify both the number of meetings *attended* and the number of meetings *missed*, for 85 per cent of the members in the union one year or over these two figures added up to twelve meetings a year or more.

question, "Why did you miss them [the meetings]?" and the answers were classified into significant categories. Involuntary reasons—such as sickness, work, being out of town—were mentioned by 26.8 per cent. Another 16.8 per cent said they had formal excuses from the shop steward. These two categories may be regarded as legitimate excuses, but they total less than half of the excuses given. The largest category (30.9 per cent) consisted of voluntary reasons for nonattendance—such as desiring to attend weddings, funerals, or ball games and having dates or parties.[3] Presumably the absentee members went to these without seeking a formal excuse. If these be counted as weaknesses on the part of members, the last large category indicates an even greater weakness on the part of the union: 20.9 per cent said they did not know about the meeting they missed until it was over. This indicates a defect in communication between the leaders and the rank and file. Less than 3 per cent said the meetings were held at an inconvenient hour.

The overwhelming majority of members do not feel that there are too many union meetings; so this is not a significant reason for nonattendance. In response to the question, "Do you think there are too many union meetings, too few, or about the right number?" only 5.1 per cent said there were too many, and a tenth of these were shop stewards who have a very high number of meetings. The largest proportion, 82.4 per cent of the total membership, said there were about the right number of meetings, and 10.7 per cent said there were not enough. (The remaining 1.8 per cent either said they did not know or gave no answer.) Clearly, a feeling that there are too many meetings is not a significant reason for nonattendance.

Participation is not only a matter of meeting attendance,

[3] Miscellaneous answers for voluntary nonattendance included "Live too far away," "bad transportation," "bad weather," "too much talking on things I'm not interested in," "other business," "no set time, don't know when they'll be from one meeting to another," "does no good to go," "I've nothing to complain about; others probably go when they want to complain," "don't like to be out alone at night."

but also of such things as speaking up from the floor at a meeting, supporting the union committee during periods of contract negotiations, reading and understanding the contract, and serving on picket lines during times of strike. The members of Local 688 report varying participation in these respects. It is probably not surprising that only a small minority speak up at union meetings (Table 4). Less than

TABLE 4. SPEAKING UP AT UNION MEETINGS

Frequency	Percentage of Members
"Usually several times a meeting"	8.9
"Once a meeting on the average"	7.9
"Only once in a while"	34.5
"Practically never"	46.4
"Don't know"; no answer	2.3
Total	100.0
Number	392

9 per cent say they speak up usually more than once per meeting, and two thirds of these are shop stewards who chair the meetings or are called upon to talk. About half the members practically never speak at union meetings. That does not mean, however, that many members feel they do not get the opportunity to talk. When asked, "Do you get a chance to say what you think in union meetings?" 83.8 per cent said, "Yes, get a good chance." Another 8.7 per cent said they get a chance if they try hard, and only 1.8 per cent said they did not get a chance. (The remainder were in the "don't know – no answer" category.)

Questions on the members' interest in union activities and on speaking up at union meetings were asked in another way: Table 5 indicates the members' opinions on these things with respect to *other members* rather than in terms of their own personal activities. Again the picture is one of high general interest in union activities, but of relatively few speaking up at meetings. The fact that the individual members' statements about themselves add up to about the same

TABLE 5. ESTIMATE BY UNION MEMBERS OF GENERAL INTEREST AND SPEAKING UP

Answer	Percentage Giving Indicated Answer to Question: "How many people in your shop are interested in union activities?"	"How many speak up at union meetings?"
"Most of them"	70.7	11.7
"About half of them"	18.7	25.5
"Very few of them"	8.7	54.9
"Don't know"; no answer	1.9	7.9
Total	100.0	100.0
Number	392	392

sort of result as their opinion about the union membership as a whole would appear to strengthen the reliability of these findings. It also suggests that most of the members have a roughly accurate idea of what is going on among the rank and file of the union. In this context it should be indicated that there is considerable variation in member interest and participation among the workers in the fifteen different companies studied.

Attendance at union meetings always competes with some other activity, usually recreational or social. An effort was made to measure the desire to participate in union meetings as against alternative ways of spending the time by asking the members the following question: "Would you rather go to a union meeting or would you rather spend your time doing something else like going to a good movie or playing cards?" The answers reveal the same desire to participate as is reflected in the figures on actual attendance already given:

49.2 per cent said, "Would rather go to a union meeting than to almost anything else."

30.1 per cent said, "Sometimes rather go to union meetings; sometimes something else."

18.4 per cent said, "Would rather do something else that I like to do."

2.3 per cent said, "Don't know," or refused to give an answer.

This is a difficult question to answer, and the reliability of the responses is uncertain. But since the answers seem to jibe with answers to other questions, and since respondents took the question seriously, the figures seem to support the impression of strong interest in union participation.

Union members were asked to estimate if the workers in their shop were strongly behind the union negotiating committee the last time there were contract negotiations with the employer. A majority of 61.1 per cent answered, "Yes, very strongly," and 25.3 per cent more said, "Yes, rather strongly." Only 5.6 per cent said, "No, not very strongly," and 1.0 per cent claimed there was hardly any support. (Another 7.0 per cent said they did not know or gave no answer, but these were predominantly new members who had not been through a period of contract negotiations.) Sixty-five per cent of the membership claimed to have read the contract between the union and the company, and about three fourths of these said they understood "all" or "most" of it.

Serving on a picket line during a strike is another activity which indicates interest and participation in the union. Two thirds of the union members said they had been on a picket line at least once. Eighteen per cent had been on a picket line only when their own shop was on strike, but 49 per cent saw service on a picket line when some other shop in the union was on strike. (The last figure includes 18.4 per cent who had been on picket lines both when their own shop was on strike and when some other shop was on strike.)

B. Participation and Evaluation of the Union

The more a member participates in his union, the more favorable is his attitude toward it. This generalization, which will be supported by facts to be offered in this section, has implications for unions everywhere in the United States. It cannot be said, of course, whether participation is the cause of high evaluation or whether high evaluation is the cause of higher participation. Nevertheless, the fact that the two are definitely associated would indicate that unions with high member participation are likely to have the greatest solidarity.

Table 6 indicates two things: (1) Most members of this union are sold on the need for a union and express satisfac-

TABLE 6. ATTENDANCE AT UNION MEETINGS AS RELATED TO UNION SOLIDARITY AND UNION CRITICISM

	Distribution of Answers by Percentage			
		Of Members Grouped by Number of Meetings Attended *		
Answer	Of All Members	6 or Fewer	7–12	Over 12
Question: "In general, what do you think of the way your union is run?"				
"Very well"	46.8	35.5	53.5	56.8
"Fairly well"	44.4	55.4	38.4	35.1
"Not so well"	3.6	5.0	4.3	2.7
"Very poorly"	3.8	4.1	3.8	2.7
"Don't know"; no answer	1.4	...	...	2.7
Total	100.0	100.0	100.0	100.0
Number	392	121	185	37
Question: "Do you think you need a union to buck the employer for you, or could you do as well by yourself?"				
"Need a union"	93.4	90.1	96.8	100.0
"Could do *almost as well* by myself"	3.1	3.3	1.6	...
"Could do *just as well* by myself"	1.5	3.3	...	...
"Could do better by myself"	0.7	1.7	...	...
"Don't know"; no answer	1.3	1.6	1.6	...
Total	100.0	100.0	100.0	100.0
Number	392	121	185	37
Question: "Are any of the union staff members not *doing a good job?"*				
"All doing a good job"	54.9	48.8	58.9	70.3
"Most doing a good job"	22.7	24.0	22.7	16.2
"About half and half"	5.6	10.7	3.8	2.7
"Most doing a poor job"	0.5	...	...	2.7
"All doing a poor job"	...	...	...	...
"Don't know"; no answer	16.3	16.5	14.6	8.1
Total	100.0	100.0	100.0	100.0
Number	392	121	185	37

* All these workers had been members of the union for at least one year

tion with union management, regardless of whether or not they attend meetings regularly. (2) The members who attend more frequently are likely to be the ones who express the strongest need for a union and who criticize the union management the least. There is a regular progression which is not only demonstrated by these figures but which is suggested more strongly when further breakdowns are made (although then the thin spread of cases makes it methodologically hazardous to place much reliance on the breakdown). It seems clear that getting members out to meetings has aided the union in getting member loyalty.

On the other hand, general loyalty does not preclude specific criticism. While the proportion of the total union membership making specific criticisms of the staff is not large,[4] there are some respects in which frequent attenders at meetings are more critical than are the infrequent attenders. A better way of stating this is that the frequent attenders are more selective in their specific criticisms: there are some matters in which more of them are critical of the staff and other matters on which very few are critical. Table 7 shows the frequent attenders of meetings to be critical in outstanding proportion in saying that the staff members are too radical or too conservative (these are two contending factions among the frequent attenders), that they are too ambitious, and that they don't carry through on the job. Only in a very low proportion do the frequent attenders say that the staff members are too lazy, too dumb, or too smart. These frequent attenders are largely shop stewards, who of course are the rank-and-file leaders of the union. Those who attend

[4] Some of the specific criticisms of the staff, volunteered in the interview and not asked about on a checklist question, include: "They lack ability," "they are not forceful enough," "they are not available when needed," "they don't attend shop meetings," "they don't help strikers," "they don't do a good job of organizing," "they don't give members a choice in some matters that come up," "they could do a better job – maybe they are bought out," "they should see to it that shop meetings are conducted properly," "got their nose in everybody's business," "they don't talk up enough," "antagonizes union members and bosses by his attitude," "refuses to give people facts," "don't have interest in members' personal problems," "doesn't give satisfactory answer to a lot of things."

TABLE 7. PROPORTIONS OF UNION MEMBERS MAKING SPECIFIC CRITICISMS OF THE STAFF, BY FREQUENCY OF ATTENDANCE AT UNION MEETINGS

	Percentage Answering Yes			
		Of Members Grouped by Number of Meetings Attended*		
Question	Of All Members	6 or Fewer	7–12	Over 12
"Are there some union staff members who:				
"are too radical	24.6	23.1	23.8	35.1
"are too conservative	18.4	24.8	13.0	27.0
"are too smart	16.1	18.2	15.1	16.2
"are too dumb	17.5	19.8	17.3	18.9
"are too ambitious	17.6	17.4	14.6	37.8
"are too lazy	14.5	16.5	13.5	13.5
"are too bossy	20.4	21.5	19.5	24.3
"don't carry through on the job?"	15.5	16.5	13.0	24.3
Number	392	121	185	37

* All these workers had been members of the union for at least one year.

regularly but not frequently (that is, those who go to from seven to twelve meetings a year) represent the backbone of the rank and file and are least critical of the staff on almost all the questions asked about the staff.

C. Members' Attitudes toward Democracy in the Union

Participation in union activities is a matter of whether or not the members believe they should be active in the union and whether or not they believe that their activity has any effect in guiding the union's policies. In other words, participation is connected with the members' belief that union democracy is desirable and that union democracy exists. We have already seen that the overwhelming majority of members of Teamsters Local 688 feel they get a chance to speak up in union meetings. In this section we shall consider further information bearing on this matter.

Three successive questions were asked about democracy in the union. The first two questions and their respective answers are presented in Table 8.[5] It will be seen that almost

[5] We use these two questions as an index of democracy even though the director and stewards are democratically elected, and leaving decisions to be

TABLE 8. EXISTENCE AND DESIRABILITY OF DEMOCRACY IN THE UNION

Answer	Percentage of Members Giving Indicated Answer to Question: "Would you rather have important matters affecting the union be decided by the union director, by the stewards' council, or by the rank-and-file members?"	"Who do you think does the deciding now?"
"The union's director"	6.6	20.2
"The stewards' council"	23.5	39.1
"The rank-and-file members"	65.6	30.2
"Don't know"; no answer	4.3	10.5
Total	100.0	100.0
Number	392	392

two thirds of the members think it desirable to have important decisions rest in the hands of rank-and-file members and that only 6.6 per cent favor having these decisions made by the union's director. Yet fewer than a third believe the rank and file makes the important decisions now, and 20.2 per cent believe the director makes them.

It might be thought that the sentiment in favor of complete democracy is a sort of pious expression of an American myth, and therefore another question was asked to place a difficult block before the choice in favor of democracy. The question was asked: "Is it more important that the top leaders of the union get what the members want and need than it is that the union be democratic, or is it more important for the union to be democratic?" The answers show that the members still choose democracy. A majority of 53.6 per cent say they feel that it is more important for the union to be

made by them might not be thought to be undemocratic. We do this because (1) some members feel that if certain important decisions are made by the director or the stewards' council, it is undemocratic; (2) attitudes toward this aspect of union organization are highly significant when related to other attitudes. Interpretation of answers to these two questions should be in terms of "more democratic and less democratic" rather than "democratic and undemocratic."

democratic than for the union to get what the members want and need; 13.5 per cent more say they don't know.

The belief that the union is and should be democratic seems to be an important stimulus to participation. Table 9

TABLE 9. RELATIONSHIP BETWEEN ATTENDANCE AT UNION MEETINGS AND VARIOUS ATTITUDES TOWARD THE CONTROL OF UNION POLICIES

	Distribution of Answers by Percentage*		
Answer as to number of meetings attended in the past year	Of those who believe union *is* and *should be* run by director or stewards' council	Of those who believe union *is* and *should be* run by rank and file	Of those who believe union *should be* run by rank and file but *is* run by director or stewards' council
None	4.0	5.7	13.9
1–2	10.5	2.3	15.9
3–6	27.6	30.3	22.8
7–12	50.0	59.4	43.6
Over 12	5.3	2.3	1.9
"Don't know"; no answer	2.6	...	1.9
Total	100.0	100.0	100.0
Number	76	101	89

* There were 13 cases of persons who believed that the union *should be* run by the director or stewards' council but *is* run by the rank and file. These are not included in the table as they are too few to present percentages on. Also not included in the table are the 52 persons who said "Don't know" or gave no answer to either question about union control; the great majority of these had been in the union only a short while and did not know who controlled policies. There were 9 other persons who gave answers but had been in the union less than a year; they are excluded because they could not have attended a full quota of meetings. The 64 shop stewards (or ex-shop stewards) are excluded because they are interested parties. The figures without these exclusions show roughly the same results, but the "purified" table presented above is much more meaningful and justifiable. (The categories mentioned in this footnote overlap slightly.)

shows that the lowest proportions of those who do not attend are found among those who believe that the union both is and should be run by the rank and file. The poorest attenders are those who feel that their democratic ideals are frustrated: among those believing that the rank and file *should* decide the important matters but that these matters *are* decided by the director or stewards' council, 29.8 per cent attend two or fewer meetings a year. This figure is to be compared with the 8.0 per cent attending two or fewer meetings a year among those saying the important matters *are* and *should be* decided by the rank and file.

Several possible divergent interpretations might be given to these facts: (1) Those who favor a democratic union but feel frustrated in their desire for democracy are thereby deterred from attending union meetings. (2) Members who are anti-union believe that no union is democratic and so see no point in attending meetings. (3) Members who are passive toward the union (neither pro- nor anti-union) express a belief that the union is undemocratic as a rationalization for their nonparticipation.

The evidence seems to give strongest support to the first possible interpretation, although the other two interpretations may have a minor validity as contributing factors. The second interpretation is weakened by the fact noted on an earlier page that very few members are anti-union in principle. Significant numbers have specific criticisms of this particular union, but only the greatest stretch of the facts would produce as many as 6 per cent who feel they do not need a union at all. The third interpretation—that the passive members rationalize their nonattendance by saying that the union is not democratic—is weakened by the data in Table 9 itself: the participation of those who want rank-and-file control but who believe control is from the top is not poor; it is simply poorer than that of other union members. Also, the attendance of those who believe control is from the top, but who are in favor of having it from the top, is very good: Only 14.5 per cent of these attend two or fewer meetings a year. Further, Table 10 shows that passive members who favor rank-and-file control are more likely than those who favor other sources of control to say "Don't know" in answer to the question about who has control at present. Thus the belief that the union is undemocratic is in itself not much of a reason for nonparticipation. Nonparticipation re-

TABLE 10. DESIRES OF UNION MEMBERS FOR DISTRIBUTION OF CONTROL AS RELATED TO THEIR BELIEFS REGARDING PRESENT DISTRIBUTION OF CONTROL

Belief regarding Actual Control	Percentage of Those with Indicated Belief Who Favor Control by: Union's Director *	Stewards' Council	Rank and File
"Control is by union's director"	63.0	17.0	16.5
"Control is by stewards' council" ...	22.2	67.1	32.7
"Control is by rank and file"........	7.4	10.6	40.6
"Don't know"; no answer	7.4	5.3	10.2
Total	100.0	100.0	100.0
Number	27	94	254

* Since only 27 persons in the sample favored control by the union's director, the percentage in this column cannot be regarded as highly reliable. It does seem justifiable, however, to note, as we do in the text, that the majority of these believe that control is currently held by the union's director and only a small proportion of them believe it is currently held by the rank and file.

sults when this belief is coupled with a desire for democracy. These facts do not disprove the third interpretation, of course. They simply weaken it, and give greater plausibility to the first interpretation.

Table 9 also suggests that the making of important decisions by the director or stewards' council is interpreted by some members as undemocratic, even though the stewards and the director achieve their position in a democratic way.[6]

Other figures show that those who are for rank-and-file control of the union, and who are satisfied that they have control, also have the greatest proportion supporting the principle of unionism and the management of this union in particular. Conversely, those who want rank-and-file control, but do not believe they have it, are relatively most critical of unionism in general and of the management of this union in particular. Of the satisfied democrats, 96.7 per cent believe

[6] Officers of Local 688 are elected by the active membership every three years. Shop stewards are elected yearly by the union members over whom they have jurisdiction. Deviations from formal democracy are: (1) The stewards' council includes staff members who are appointed rather than elected. (2) The stewards' council may dismiss a shop steward without the consent of the members in his shop. (This last rule was not adopted until spring, 1949, and was not employed while the survey was in progress.)

a union is necessary and 60.0 per cent think their union is run very well. But of the dissatisfied democrats, only 87.5 per cent believe a union is necessary and 38.6 per cent think their union is run very well.[7]

From all the data presented in this section we may draw the conclusion that the large attendance at union meetings and the strong union loyalty rest partly on the strong desire for union democracy among a majority of the members. The minority that feel frustrated in their desire for democracy in the union are the poorest attenders, and it is likely that their attendance and their loyalty to the union could be increased if their conception of union democracy were more fully realized.

Table 10 analyzes further the nature of the attitude toward democracy in the union. The majority of those who favor control by the union's director or by the shop stewards believe that control is vested in these persons (63.0 per cent and 67.1 per cent, respectively). Similarly, the largest proportion (40.6 per cent) of those who favor control by the rank and file believe the latter actually do have control. All these persons may be said to be satisfied with the organization of control in the union. Few of the members think there is more control lodged in the rank and file than there should be (only 7.4 per cent of those who favor control by the director, and 10.6 per cent of those who favor control by the stewards, believe that control actually is held by the rank and file). Those who favor control by the rank and file, but believe that the control actually lies elsewhere, are more inclined to believe that the control is held by the stewards' council than by the director. That is, this large group of dissatisfied persons, insofar as they resent what they believe to be the lack of democracy in the union, contains twice as many people who feel resentment toward the stewards' council as toward the union's director.

[7] Those who believe the union both *is* and *should be* run by the director or the stewards' council — who may be called the satisfied nondemocrats — are in between the other two groups on all counts.

D. Probing into the Causes of Solidarity

Although thus far in this chapter our particular subjects have been union participation and attitudes toward democracy, many of the facts reported have provided evidence of worker solidarity. The most significant finding already mentioned is that 93.4 per cent of the members say they need a union and only 2.2 per cent say they could do just as well or better by themselves.[8] While certainly no claim could be made that this is a typical union, it should not be thought that the workers are so enthusiastic about the principle of unionism because they once were without a union and therefore knew how to appreciate it when it came. At the time of the survey all the *shops* studied had been in the union *at least* seven years, and yet three fifths of the *membership* studied had not been in the union that long. When asked the question, "Why did you join the union?" the indicated proportions gave the answers presented in Table 11. Apparently almost half the members (those giving reasons 1 and 8) think of themselves as having joined the union involuntarily. Another very large proportion (those giving reasons 2 and 3) give only general and vague reasons for having joined the union. Only a tiny proportion (2.8 per cent) give a reason ("The majority wanted it") that might be interpreted as anti-unionism.

It would seem from these facts that the experience con-

[8] That this figure is not fallaciously high or an artifact of our method is shown by the equally high proportions of workers generally in favor of union shops in secret ballot elections conducted by the National Labor Relations Board under the provisions of the Taft-Hartley Act. In a study of local unions in Buffalo, New York, for example, employers and outside observers alike were surprised by the conclusions. "In only two of the 127 elections studied did a majority of the eligible votes fail to authorize a union shop. Over ninety-six per cent of the workers who voted in the elections cast 'yes' ballots. More than ninety-one per cent of those who were eligible to participate did vote." (Horace E. Sheldon, *Union Security and the Taft-Hartley Act in the Buffalo Area* [Ithaca: New York State School of Industrial and Labor Relations, 1949], p. 37.) In Teamsters Local 688, the proportions in favor of the union in the NLRB elections ranged from 94 to 98 per cent for the various shops. (*Midwest Labor World*, September 27, 1950, p. 1.)

TABLE 11. REASONS FOR JOINING THE UNION

Reason Given	Percentage of Members *
1. "Had to – I work in a union shop"	45.9
2. "For my own benefit" (general, but personal)	20.9
3. "It is a good cause" (general, but impersonal)	16.3
4. "For higher wages"	7.7
5. "For better working conditions"	6.6
6. "For security"	4.3
7. "There is strength in numbers"	3.3
8. "The majority wanted it"	2.8
9. No answer	1.3
Number	392

* The figures add up to more than 100 per cent because a person could give more than one answer.

nected with *joining* the union did not produce the loyalty to the principle of unionism. The alternative possibilities are that (1) the union members had a sense of general union solidarity *before* joining the union; (2) the members developed a sense of union solidarity as a result of their experiences in this union. While the first undoubtedly occurred in some cases, we believe the latter interpretation to be the more significant. From what is generally known about the mildly unfavorable attitudes toward unions on the part of nonunion members in the United States, it is likely that most of the young, unskilled workers going into the union during the past seven years did not have very strong attitudes of union loyalty before joining the union. We may fairly assume, then, that most of the new members went in without knowing much about the union and having relatively neutral attitudes toward it. The strong union solidarity that we discover evidence of probably comes mostly from experiences in the union. Certainly we know that those experiences cannot possibly have materially reduced the solidarity.

We have already analyzed attendance at union meetings as a probable source of solidarity. The union formerly fined members for nonattendance, but for two years prior to the survey this was not done because of the Taft-Hartley Act. A belief that the important union decisions should be made by the rank-and-file members seems, on the basis of facts presented in the previous section, to be a motivation for attending meetings and thus indirectly is a cause of the high solidarity.

But this is only one side of the picture, and possibly the less significant side in terms of workers' motivations. Another very significant set of facts comes out of the answers to the question, "What do you consider to be the purposes of your union? (What is a union for?)" Interviewers did not prompt the respondents on answers to this question, but allowed them to answer just as they pleased. After a union member had given all the purposes of a union he had in mind, the interviewer inquired as to how well he thought the union accomplished each of them. The distribution of purposes given and of evaluations for each purpose are presented in Table 12.

The table shows that members get a wide range of benefits from union membership. Getting higher wages (or the equivalent) stands out in most workers' minds as the most important purpose of a union, of course, but substantial proportions spontaneously mentioned getting job security, gaining rights, and getting benefits off the job (such as opportunities for recreation, medical care, and legal advice). Needless to say, these things are important to workers, and if they feel the union is getting these things for them, they are convinced that unionism is necessary. The figures on the right-hand side of the table show that very few members feel that the union is not accomplishing its purposes. For all the purposes given, those saying that these purposes are accomplished poorly or not at all range from 0 per cent to 6.2 per cent.[9] The union is felt to accomplish some purposes "un-

[9] The 6.2 per cent refers to the purpose "getting benefits off the job." We shall see later that members are pleased with the medical benefits they get by being in the union, and this is probably reflected in the fact that a majority of the members feel the union accomplishes this purpose "unusually well." Since the union has practically no recreation program, it is probably this weakness which partly causes the relatively large amount of criticism. Another cause is probably that some members do not get medical benefits.

TABLE 12. OPINIONS OF UNION MEMBERS ON WHAT THE PURPOSES OF THE UNION ARE AND HOW WELL THESE ARE ACCOMPLISHED

Purpose Mentioned	Percentage of Members Mentioning *	Number of Mentions	Percentage of Those Mentioning Who Gave Indicated Reply to Question: "How well accomplished?"						
			"Unusually well"	"Pretty well"	"Average"	"Fairly poorly"	"Not at all"	"Don't know"; No Answer	Total
"Get specific economic benefits" (higher wages)	75.3	462	39.4	41.8	15.8	1.7	...	1.3	100.0
"Get job security" (including seniority)	31.1	133	51.1	39.8	5.3	0.7	0.8	2.3	100.0
"Gain rights" (e.g., "welfare," free speech, fair deal)	16.6	67	34.3	49.3	7.5	...	3.0	5.9	100.0
"Get benefits off the job" (recreational, medical, legal)	10.7	48	52.1	27.1	14.6	2.1	4.1	...	100.0
"Organize labor; get solidarity for bargaining"	9.4	41†	29.3	41.5	17.1	4.8	...	...	100.0
"Raise the standard of living"	7.9	32†	53.1	37.5	4.4	...	...	...	100.0
"Make labor and management more cooperative"	5.1	21†	52.4	38.1	4.8	4.7	...	...	100.0
"Increase fellowship among workers"	3.8	15†	33.3	33.4	33.3	...	...	...	100.0
Miscellaneous; "don't know"; no answer ...	2.6	12†	...	...	...	...	...	...	100.0

* The figures in this column add up to more than 100 per cent because a person could give more than one answer.
† This number is too small to permit much reliability in the percentage distributions.

usually well" by a majority of the members: getting job security, getting benefits off the job, raising the standard of living, and making labor and management more cooperative. The union comes in for the most criticism relatively in the matters of organizing new shops and of raising wages.[10] On the whole, however, the members feel that the union is performing a successful job in getting many important services accomplished.

Another most significant evidence of solidarity in this particular union and of the feeling that the union is satisfying a major need appears in answers to the question, "Since you are a member of a union, do you feel that your boss can't push you around as much as he might want to?" A large majority (71.7 per cent) of the members apparently get a sense of security about their jobs because of the union, and only 4.6 per cent feel that the union fails completely in preventing arbitrary action on the part of the employer. (Another 21.7 per cent took the intermediate position that "The union helps some, but not completely," and 2 per cent gave no answer.)

As we shall see in the following chapter, members do not hesitate to criticize specific union policies with which they happen to disagree. The large proportions of members expressing satisfaction with the union's accomplishments thus seem to be reliable facts. Satisfaction with the union's achievements would intrinsically appear to be an important basis of the high solidarity.

Contributory to the union solidarity of the members of this particular union is the general support given to unions by most people in the working class. It might almost be said that belonging to a union is now "traditional" for a large portion of the workers. This is illustrated by the figures in Table 13. Over three fifths of the members report that their

[10] There also appears to be noteworthy criticism about the union's achievement in promoting fellowship among members. But since this purpose was mentioned by so few persons, the proportions should not be considered reliable.

TABLE 13. FAMILY SUPPORT FOR MEMBERS' UNION AFFILIATION

Answer to Question: "Is your family in favor of your belonging to a union?"	Distribution of Answers by Percentage		
		Of Those Saying Union Is Run:	
	Of All Members	"Very well"	"Fairly well"
"Yes, they approve strongly"	62.8	71.4	55.5
"Yes, they approve mildly"	12.5	10.7	13.3
"They don't care either way"	19.9	13.8	26.1
"No, they disapprove mildly"	1.3	1.0	1.1
"No, they disapprove strongly"	1.3	1.0	1.1
No answer	2.2	2.1	2.9
Total	100.0	100.0	100.0
Number	392	188	173

families strongly approve their affiliation with a union, and 12.5 per cent more say their families approve mildly. Only 2.6 per cent report their families opposed to union affiliation. Another question asked was whether anyone in the members' families had ever belonged to a union, and about three fourths (74.0 per cent) answered "Yes." These reported an average of 1.6 relatives in a union at one time or another (and most members reported only for their immediate families, not their collateral relatives).[11] These overwhelming figures indicate that the members of Local 688 live in a social milieu favorable to unionism generally. The members are thus predisposed to exhibit union solidarity. The connection between family approval and the members' own evaluation of the way the union is run is indicated in the last part of Table 13. While family disapproval makes no differences, strong family approval is related to greater enthusiasm for the way the union is run.

E. Attitudes toward the Employers

The question may be raised as to whether the high degree of worker solidarity is associated with antagonism toward

[11] Twenty-six per cent reported that their spouse is or had been a member of the union; 29.1 per cent mentioned parent or parents; 29.3 per cent mentioned sibling or siblings; 11.5 per cent mentioned offspring; 8.2 per cent mentioned other relatives.

the employer. In other words, is there a "class struggle" in the minds of the workers so that the large number of strongly pro-union workers are anti-employer? The evidence which arises from this study seems to suggest that there is no inflexible antagonism toward employers on the part of the large majority of workers. If anything, the evidence supports

TABLE 14. INDICATIONS OF ATTITUDES OF UNION MEMBERS TOWARD THEIR EMPLOYERS

Answer	Percentage of Members
Question: "How do your union staff leaders get along with your employer?"	
"Give in too much to the employer"	4.4
"Just about right: they push hard enough for us, but are also fair to the employer"	88.0
"The union is sometimes unfair to the employer"	3.3
"Don't know"; no answer	4.3
Total	100.0
Number	392
Question: "Is it just as wrong for a worker to file a grievance which is not permitted by his contract as it is for a boss to break a contract?"	
"Yes"	76.0
"No"	6.4
"It depends" *	13.8
"Don't know"; no answer	3.8
Total	100.0
Number	392

* Answers specifying what "it depends" on include: "on the grievance," "on the situation," "on the contract," "on many things."

the opposite contention that the union movement is a buttress for the free enterprise system. Workers *do* fear arbitrary treatment and dismissal by the employer, and there is consequently some hostility. But since the union provides protection against such arbitrary action, the "class struggle" mentality has not developed for the great majority of the workers. Their position seems to be that the union should protect them against employers, but that the union should also be fair to employers. This attitude is best revealed in answers to the first question in Table 14. Only 4.4 per cent are in favor of an aggressive anti-employer policy. On the

TABLE 15. OPINIONS OF UNION MEMBERS REGARDING THE FAIRNESS OF EMPLOYERS, AND THE RELATIONSHIP BETWEEN THESE OPINIONS AND THE DESIRE OF THE MEMBERS TO BE FAIR TO THE EMPLOYER

Answer	Distribution of Answers by Percentage		
		Of Members with Indicated Attitude toward Grievances against Contract	
	Of All Members	Not in Favor	In Favor or Saying "It depends"
Question: "Do you think your foreman is fair to the workers?"			
"Very fair most of the time"	72.2	72.7	68.0
"Sometimes fair, sometimes not fair"	21.9	21.6	25.6
"Hardly ever fair"	4.8	4.7	5.1
"Don't know"; no answer	1.1	1.0	1.3
Total	100.0	100.0	100.0
Number	392	298	79
Question: "Do you think the top officials and bosses of the company are fair to the workers?"			
"Very fair most of the time"	50.0	50.7	47.4
"Sometimes fair, sometimes not fair"	27.8	28.0	32.0
"Hardly ever fair"	3.6	3.7	2.6
"Don't know because I never have any contact with them"	18.4	17.3	18.0
No answer	0.2	0.3	...
Total	100.0	100.0	100.0
Number	392	298	79

other hand, only 3.3 per cent say that the union is sometimes unfair to the employer.[12]

The matter of fairness to the employer is dealt with by the first question in Table 14 in a sort of general way. The second question in the table deals with it in a highly specific way. Three fourths of the workers indicate a strict sense of fairness toward the employer, and most of the others only want to make the fairness conditional.

Just as important as the workers' desire to be fair to the employer is their conception of whether or not employers are fair to them. The two are only slightly related, as Table 15

[12] Kinds of unfairness to the employer mentioned by some members include: "demand things that are silly, like getting off on your birthday"; "uphold a lazy person, even one who steals and is caught"; "the employee is sometimes wrong"; "union is only 75 per cent right in grievances."

shows. This table presents the strongest evidence that a "class conflict" does not exist in the minds of the workers, despite the strong support for the union and the even higher loyalty to the principle of unionism. Only 3.6 per cent say the top officials of the company are hardly ever fair (slightly more—4.8 per cent—feel that the foreman is hardly ever fair). Just as striking is the smallness of the relationship to the question of abiding by the contract. Even those who are not always in favor of abiding by the contract are hardly more inclined than the others are to believe the employer unfair.

Another specific issue on which worker fairness to employers can be measured is whether wage demands can constantly be made on employers. Some employers are fearful of unions because they believe the unions will drive up wages beyond the point at which they can remain in business. Some union leaders have the same worry in another form: Will their rank-and-file members insist that wages be constantly increased (which under some circumstances becomes impossible), and if they fail to raise wages will the rank and file desert the union? Evidence from this study indicates that neither fear is justified. Table 16 shows that only a small minority (10.7 per cent) of the members of this union expect to get increases in pay indefinitely. Furthermore, there is no relationship between this expectation and whether or not the workers think the employer is fair. It is only those who do not know about the fairness of the employer because they have no contact with him who differ markedly from the average. They are the ones who most expect future wage increases to depend on business conditions and who least expect the union to get wage increases indefinitely.

Since a belief in the fairness of top company officials is not related to an expectation of indefinite wage increases, we once more have evidence that loyalty to a workers' movement does not conflict with a sense of accommodation to the employer. In summary, only a tiny minority in this union

TABLE 16. RELATIONSHIP BETWEEN THE ATTITUDES OF UNION MEMBERS TOWARD FUTURE WAGE INCREASES AND THEIR ATTITUDES TOWARD THE FAIRNESS OF EMPLOYERS

	Distribution of Answers by Percentage			
		Of Members with Indicated Estimate of Fairness of Top Company Officials		
Answer	Of All Members	"Very fair most of the time"	"Sometimes unfair" or "Hardly ever fair"	"Don't know because no contact with them"
Question: "If your union is strong enough, will it always be able to get wage increases, or will there come a time soon when the employer can't afford wage increases?"				
"Yes, the union can get anything if it works hard enough"	10.7	12.6	12.3	2.8
"No, there is a limit to what the employer can or will pay"	27.0	28.8	31.1	14.1
"Depends on how business conditions are and whether prices go up some more"	54.3	49.5	52.5	71.8
"Don't know"	7.7	8.6	4.1	11.3
No answer	0.3	0.5	...	...
Total	100.0	100.0	100.0	100.0
Number	392 *	196	123	72

* The total includes one person who did not respond to the question about the top officials of the company.

have a "class struggle" mentality. Such a mentality is therefore not a significant support of the strong union loyalty.[13]

F. Summary

1. There is a good deal of member participation in the activities of Teamsters Local 688, in terms of attending meetings, supporting negotiating committees during periods of

[13] A study of workers' attitudes in another union corroborates our finding that there is no conflict in workers' minds between their loyalty to the union and to the company. The other union is a large CIO union in a single large plant, near a city which has the reputation of being much more liberal than St. Louis. Since this other union is in such different circumstances from our own, it would seem that our findings here have general applicability. (See Benjamin Willerman, "Group Identification in Industry," unpublished Ph.D. thesis, Massachusetts Institute of Technology, 1949.)

contract negotiations, reading and understanding the contract, and serving on picket lines during times of strike. Only a minority, however, speak up regularly at union meetings. Unexcused nonattendance at meetings is apparently due not only to alternative attractions (social and recreational) but also to the failure of the union to let some members know when meetings are to be held.

2. Practically all the members of the union are convinced that a union is necessary, even though most of them acknowledge coming into the union involuntarily (because they got jobs in a union shop). Their worker solidarity and their loyalty to this union in particular seem to rest on two bases: (a) their high degree of participation in union activities (coupled with a desire for democratic control); (b) their feeling that the union is successful in achieving its purposes —purposes which are important to them as workers.

3. Loyalty to the union does not preclude criticism of specific policies or of specific union leaders. In fact, the more active participants in union activities are the ones who are most critical on selected counts.

4. A desire for democracy in the union is one factor back of the high participation. No doubt the encouragement given by union leaders to rank-and-file participation, and the enforced (by fine) participation before the Taft-Hartley Act, are also contributory factors. Those whose desire for democracy is frustrated, because they believe that major union policies are set by the director or the stewards' council rather than by the rank and file, are relatively the poorest attenders at union meetings.

5. Antagonism toward employers as such, or a "class struggle" mentality, is very minor in the union. Thus this could not be a basis of the high union loyalty. The workers want to be fair to the employers (just as most of them believe the employers are usually fair to them), so that neither employers nor union leaders have to worry about compromising on wage increases when the employers reach the limit of what they can pay and still remain in business.

CHAPTER IV

The Extent to Which Members Agree with Union Policies

We have seen that the members of Teamsters Local 688 regard their union as rather successful in achieving its goals with respect to the employers and the general outside world. This, of course, is considered a major success by the union leaders. But the leadership also feels that it must secure certain attitudes among the rank-and-file members. Such attitudes are deemed to be necessary for the successful running of a union. Therefore success of the leaders' policies must also be measured by the proportions of the members who hold these attitudes.

The first objectives of the leadership of any organization in regard to the attitudes of the rank and file must be to gain loyal support and willingness to participate. In the last chapter we noted that the membership of this union had a good measure of these basic requirements. But we now need to delve further into attitudes toward specific union policies. The author of this study does not take an attitude toward these specific policies, either as to whether they are intrinsically good or bad, or as to whether they are ultimately helpful or harmful to the union movement. Suffice it to say, for the purposes of this study, that the union leadership regards certain attitudes on the part of the rank and file as necessary or desirable for the achievement of the union's purposes, and it seeks to inculcate such attitudes. The success or failure of the union in inculcating these specific attitudes is the subject of this chapter.

It is not only the leadership, of course, that is the source of the attitudes. Probably union experiences, especially in times of crisis, are of even greater influence as a teacher. One experience with the "speed-up" does more than dozens of speeches to teach workers to oppose incentive pay. One period of laying-off due to economic recession is more effective than scores of arguments to get workers behind the seniority principle. "A strike is the best education," say experienced union officials. Not only do union experiences educate directly, but they provide the teaching aids by means of which the older members educate the newer ones. Union indoctrination is not only an aim of the union leaders, but of the experienced rank and file as well.

The general effect of all this education and indoctrination is to build solidarity in the union. In this chapter we shall consider solidarity in terms of specific attitudes toward union policies which can be measured.

A. Attitudes toward Incentive Pay

One specific attitude fostered as a principle of unionism is that a weekly wage (or its equivalent) is preferable to piecework pay. The remuneration of workers according to their output is said to lead to the "speed-up" (whereby employers exact more and more production from the workers without ultimately giving them more pay) and to a division of interests between less efficient and more efficient workers. Many employers like incentive pay, on the other hand, because they feel it encourages initiative and ability as well as increases output.[1]

A question on this subject was asked in the survey of union members, and the results are shown in Table 17. The members are about evenly divided for and against monetary

[1] In some industries piecework is so difficult to measure that incentive pay is not feasible. This tends to be true among the warehouse workers of Local 688, but not among the manufacturing workers, for whom incentive pay is feasible.

TABLE 17. ATTITUDES OF UNION MEMBERS TOWARD BONUSES AND PIECEWORK PAY

Answer	Distribution of Answers by Percentage: Of All Members	Of Members Grouped by Number of Meetings Attended in Past Year *: 6 or Fewer	7–12	Over 12
Question: "What do you think of bonuses, piecework pay, and other rewards for harder work?"				
"Like them"	41.1	47.1	33.0	24.3
"Don't like them"	41.3	38.0	47.0	64.9
"Don't care either way"	14.0	13.2	15.7	8.1
"Don't know"; no answer	3.6	1.7	4.3	2.7
Total	100.0	100.0	100.0	100.0
Number	392	121	185	37

* All these workers had been members of the union for at least one year.

rewards for harder work.[2] We do not know what the proportions would have been when the union was in its infancy, so we have no basis of comparison for determining in that way whether the union leadership has been successful or not in its member-education program. There is another kind of evidence, however, that the member-education program is having some effect. Those who attend union meetings more frequently are much more likely to be against the incentives for harder work. This is not proof, of course, since it may be that the motivation which makes people vote against incentive pay is also the motivation which brings them out to meetings, so that member personality rather than leadership efforts is the major factor. But the simpler explanation seems to be in terms of the efforts of leaders and older members.

B. *Attitudes toward Job Seniority*

Another specific policy which this union shares with other unions is that workers should be promoted in strict accordance with the length of time they have been on the job, and

[2] Interviewers were instructed to indicate that this question did not refer to Christmas bonuses, which are in the nature of a general gift rather than an individual reward for greater effort. Still, some of the workers may have thought that the question applied to Christmas bonuses as well, and if this is true, the proportion indicated as being in favor of rewards for harder work is unduly high.

that if there must be layoffs, those most recently hired must be the ones fired first. This is the principle of job seniority. Unions feel it is necessary to prevent arbitrary action on the part of employers, and so prevent employers from firing a worker for union activity on the pretense that he is not efficient. They also hold that job seniority is necessary to protect older workers when other companies would not hire them. Thus union leaders feel that job seniority is an absolute essential in firing. Many leaders feel that job seniority is necessary to build up a core of members who are solidly loyal to the union and to prevent the employer from exercising his personal whims in making promotions, and so these leaders insist on the principle of job seniority in promotion also. The leadership of Teamsters Local 688 believes in both kinds of job seniority.

Those employers who are against the principle of job seniority feel that it discourages the workers with ability and initiative, since promotion results not from these qualities but solely from length of tenure on the job. They also feel it reduces output, especially when they have to fire a capable young man and hold onto a much less satisfactory worker.

Still another criticism of job seniority in promotion, expressed by a few union leaders and several outside observers of the union movement, is that it tends to divide the members when older workers can "bump" the younger ones in times of job scarcity. This is said to be especially serious when high seniority workers, with high hourly rates of pay, work for three or four days a week at their own jobs and then displace workers with lower hourly rates of pay for the remaining two or three days. In this case the high seniority worker not only earns as much during his three or four days as the low seniority worker could earn in five or six, but he is also able to take away work days from the latter.

Three fourths (76.3 per cent) of the workers approve job seniority in both promotions and layoffs. Only 7.1 per cent are against it completely, and only a third of these specify that they would substitute "ability" for it as the basis of promotions and layoffs. A sizable minority of 15.6 per cent would have promotions and layoffs be made sometimes on the basis of seniority, sometimes on some other basis. In this group are 6.9 per cent who are willing to use the principle of job seniority only when the workers involved have equal ability, 4.1 per cent who favor seniority in layoffs but ability on promotions, and 4.6 per cent who do not specify their partial substitute for seniority. On the whole, the union members seem to support job seniority. Even among the workers with less than one year's seniority, 68.2 per cent are in favor of it.

C. Attitudes toward Organizing the Unorganized

A basic principle of most unions is to get as many shops into the union as possible, so that the employer whose shop is organized will not have a competitive disadvantage as compared to an employer whose shop is not organized, and so that the former cannot plead this competitive disadvantage as a basis for refusing to raise wages. In some industries the unorganized shops serve as a source of "scabs" who can be used to break the union in organized shops, but this does not apply to Teamsters Local 688, since most of the workers are unskilled anyway and it is easy to find "scabs." Still other motives for organization are to extend the benefits of the union to more workers and to extend the power of union leaders.

Organization takes time and money. Since this is largely staff members' time (paid for out of union dues) and the money comes directly out of the union treasury, there is also a motivation for the individual union member not to encourage too much organization. Two questions were asked on the survey to get at this matter, and the answers are shown in Table 18. On the first question, it is apparent that the overwhelming majority of the membership subscribes in principle to organizing the unorganized. Only 6.9 per cent of the members believe that very little or none of the union's time and money should be devoted to organization.

TABLE 18. ATTITUDES OF UNION MEMBERS TOWARD SPENDING TIME AND MONEY ON NEW ORGANIZATION

Answer	Percentage of Members
Question: "How much time and money should your union put into organizing workers in places where there is no union now?"	
"A great deal"	37.8
"Some"	47.4
"Very little"	4.3
"None at all"	2.6
"Don't know"; no answer	6.4
Total	100.0
Number	392
Question: "Should your union put more time and money into unionizing these nonunion places or should it put more into getting more and better things for the people already in the union?"	
"More into new organizational drives"	30.6
"More into working for present union members"	32.1
"About the same amount"	35.0
No answer	2.3
Total	100.0
Number	392

When it comes to a realistic alternative, however, opinions are somewhat different. The number of those who favor spending more time and money on new organizational drives than on working for present union members is roughly about the same as the number who prefer the opposite distribution of time and money—about a third of the total membership in each group. The last third compromised by saying there should be equal expenditures for the two purposes. Although the members' support for organizational drives is not so great on the second question as on the first one, it is still quite considerable. The union leaders' aim of getting membership backing for new organizational drives, therefore, seems to be achieved in large measure.[3]

There is a role in new organization which the ordinary member can play without its costing him any money. This

[3] This attitude may have changed since the survey was in the field, since the union has since then failed in a major organizational drive, in which a great deal of time and money was spent. When a strike fund was being debated shortly thereafter, many of the members wanted to prohibit the expenditure of any of the fund for organizational purposes.

TABLE 19. WILLINGNESS OF UNION MEMBERS TO PICKET SOME OTHER SHOP

Answer	Distribution of Answers by Percentage					
	Of All Members	Of Shop Stewards	Of Nonstewards, Grouped by Years in Union			
			Less than 1	1–3	4–10	Over 10
Question: "Are you willing to picket to help some other shop get organized or get a raise in pay?"						
"Yes"	79.1	95.3	61.4	73.0	79.6	90.3
"No"	18.4	3.1	31.8	24.3	19.8	9.7
"Don't know"; no answer	2.5	1.6	6.8	2.7	0.6	...
Total	100.0	100.0	100.0	100.0	100.0	100.0
Number	392 *	64	44	74	172	31

* The total includes seven persons who did not respond to the question about longevity in the union.

is walking in a picket line around the unorganized shop to encourage the workers in it to join the union and to discourage nonmembers from working in the shop. Almost 80 per cent of the members would be willing to picket for a shop other than their own, as Table 19 indicates, and only 18.4 per cent say they would not be willing to do so.[4] Furthermore, willingness to picket is in direct proportion to length of membership in the union, which is not true for the other two questions regarding the spending of union money and staff time on new organization.[5] Whereas only 61.4 per cent of the members who have been in the union less than a year are willing to picket, 90.3 per cent of the oldest members are willing, as are 95.3 per cent of the shop stewards. Here again is strong evidence of success in achieving a certain attitude among the members.

D. Stimulating Interest in Broader Issues, Including Politics

More than ever in the past few years, union leaders have come to believe that it is necessary for workers to become

[4] The question asks about picketing not only for new organization but also for getting a raise in pay for the existing membership. It may not, therefore, exactly reflect the point made above.

[5] The characteristics of the older members as compared to the newer are presented in Chapter VII, Section A.

interested in and exercise their influence in politics and other issues outside their immediate shop.[6] The leaders have been accused of desiring to extend their own personal power because of this. But they claim that the gains of workers won by collective bargaining, strikes, and other means of direct economic attack are jeopardized by certain laws, and these laws are made by elected representatives of the people. Therefore, they say, workers need to express themselves in politics in order to elect legislators or convince them to vote against antilabor legislation and for prolabor legislation. In other words, the expansion of the realm of law to cover many matters of vital economic interest to workers has made political action necessary. The leaders of Teamsters Local 688 believe strongly in political action.

The matter is, in one sense, an extension of the problem considered in the previous section. The union leaders want to get the rank-and-file members to understand not only that the organization of the unorganized is for their own benefit, but that the organization of all workers for political action is also for their own benefit. In other words, the union leaders want to get the rank and file to see that their economic interests extend beyond their shop.

The first question asked on the subject in the survey puts the matter on this immediate basis. The question, reported in Table 20, is not a good one from a technical standpoint because it is ambiguous. Still, the answers have some interest, especially when we make a comparison between members with different lengths of membership in the union. Among all the members 62.2 per cent indicated they had some interest in union problems outside their own shops, but 23.2 per cent said they had no interest at all (and 13.0

[6] The industrial unions long held this attitude, and the CIO went so far as to form a Political Action Committee (PAC) in 1944, with the direct purpose of influencing elections. The craft unions avoided politics as a matter of principle for a long time, but gradually took an increasing interest as they saw more labor issues being decided by the government. When Congress passed the Taft-Hartley Act in 1947, which practically all union leaders regard as anti-union, the AF of L formed a Labor's League for Political Education (LLPE).

TABLE 20. RELATIONSHIP BETWEEN INTERESTS OUTSIDE THE SHOP AND LONGEVITY

Answer	Distribution of Answers by Percentage					
			Of Nonstewards, Grouped by Years in Union			
	Of All Members	Of Shop Stewards	Less than 1	1–3	4–10	Over 10
Question: "Do union problems which do not *concern your shop interest you?"* *						
"Yes, very much"	27.4	51.6	11.4	13.5	29.1	29.0
"Yes, somewhat"	34.8	32.8	34.1	41.9	32.0	38.7
"No, only very occasionally"	13.0	9.4	18.2	14.9	12.8	6.5
"No, not at all"	23.2	6.2	34.1	27.0	25.6	25.8
"Don't know"; no answer	1.5	...	2.2	2.7	0.5	...
Total	100.0	100.0	100.0	100.0	100.0	100.0
Number	392	64	44	74	172	31

* If the union members asked what was referred to by the question, the interviewers were instructed to answer, "Such things as getting more union members, labor politics, etc."

per cent more said they were not interested except occasionally). Those who had a long membership in the union expressed considerably more interest in union problems outside their shop than did the newcomers: 29 per cent of those who had been members at least four years said they were very much interested, compared to only 11.4 per cent among those who had been members less than one year. The shop stewards expressed most interest, of course. There were, however, as many as 15.6 per cent of them who expressed little or no interest in union matters outside their shop.[7] On the whole, it would seem that the longer the experience in the union, the broader the interests the members have. Members who expressed interest in union matters outside their shop explained their interest in terms of making the union stronger, of expressing a common concern of all workers, or of helping themselves in the long run.

[7] Since shop stewards make up the equivalent of a legislature for the union as a whole, they are obliged to attend to matters outside their shop at least once a month. The 15.6 per cent may consist of former shop stewards rather than the present ones, since the survey provides no way of distinguishing between these two categories.

A whole series of questions asked of the union members brings out directly their attitudes toward the union's participation in politics. The first puts up again the realistic hurdle of time and money, which engaging in politics would require. Table 21 shows that almost a third say the union

TABLE 21. ATTITUDES OF UNION MEMBERS TOWARD TWO TYPES OF UNION ACTIVITY

Answer	Percentage Giving Indicated Answer to Question: "How much time and money should your union put into getting candidates elected to public office who are friendly to labor?"	Percentage Giving Indicated Answer to Question: "How much time and money should your union put into organizing workers in places where there is no union now?"
"A great deal"	30.6	37.8
"Some"	48.7	47.4
"Very little"	7.9	4.3
"None at all"	7.1	2.6
"Don't know"; no answer	5.7	7.9
Total	100.0	100.0
Number	392	392

should put "a great deal" of time and money into getting candidates who are friendly to labor elected to public office, and another 48.7 per cent would favor the union's spending "some time and money." While these are large proportions, they are not so high as those favoring the union's spending time and money on organizational campaigns. It would seem, then, that the membership is convinced of the need for political activity, but not quite so much as for organizational activity.

When unions engage in political action, they not only use union funds but also urge their members to contribute extra money for this purpose. Before the Taft-Hartley Act of 1947, some unions used their funds directly and required extra assessments (usually $1) from their members for political action. Since that became illegal, the unions have encouraged their members to make voluntary contributions to a political action committee controlled by union leaders but formally only loosely affiliated with the unions. The survey included the following question on voluntary contributions for political action: "During an election year, how much money would you be willing to give in order to help candidates friendly to labor?" The distribution of answers is as follows:

Answer	*Percentage*
"Nothing"	22.5
$ .01–.99	.3
$1.00	8.2
$1.01–2.00	6.1
Over $2.00	11.2
"Something" (unspecified amount)	23.7
"Don't know"	16.6
No answer	11.4
Total	100.0

It would seem from these figures that the members are not enthusiastic about these contributions. Only 11.2 per cent indicate that they would be willing to give over $2.00. A majority could be found to contribute $1.00 voluntarily (although this is determined from answers to another question rather than to this one). The absence of any great willingness on the part of union members to contribute extra money for political action would appear to be a limitation on the union's activity in that direction.

Money is not so important as influence for political action, however, and the evidence of the survey suggests that the union leaders are very influential in forming the political attitudes of the members. The first question asked members on this subject was whether they voted in the 1948 election for president. In the sample studied, 63.5 per cent said they had. For St. Louis City as a whole, about 52.9 per cent of the total population voted.[8] These two figures are not exactly

[8] The figure for St. Louis City was courteously provided by Dr. David Salmon from an unpublished study by Edward Olds and David Salmon.

comparable,[9] of course, but if the members are answering honestly, the figures would still indicate that union members voted in greater proportion than St. Louisans as a whole.

Additional evidence of heavier voting among union people comes from the fact that 53.4 per cent of union members with either husbands or wives said that their spouses voted. A further question, asked of those who voted, was, "Would you mind saying for whom you voted?" While all but 6.8 per cent of those who said they voted named the presidential candidate for whom they claimed to have voted, other studies[10] suggest that answers to such a question are not too reliable. Some people like to say that they picked the winner even if they did not. Nevertheless, the figures arising out of this survey are so overwhelmingly one-sided that they do indicate the presidential candidate favored by at least a substantial majority:

Answer	*Percentage*
Truman	81.5
Dewey	9.3
Wallace	.8
Thomas	.4
Others	1.2
"Won't say"	6.8
Total	100.0

It is probable that most of those who did not answer voted either for Dewey or for Wallace. Although a substantial majority of people with low incomes, poor educational background, etc., voted for Truman, the St. Louis wards where most of these people live did not return quite so high a pro-

[9] The two figures are not comparable because (1) some of the city's population is institutionalized and therefore not capable of voting; (2) some of the union members do not live in St. Louis City, but in St. Louis County and adjacent territory; (3) the age distribution of the union membership is on the younger side as compared to the city as a whole, and younger people usually vote more frequently than do older people; (4) two thirds of the union membership is male, as compared with about 50 per cent for the city as a whole, and men usually vote more frequently than do women; (5) most important of all, about 7 per cent of the union membership was under voting age in 1948, and so was ineligible to vote.

[10] For example, the unpublished study directed by Dr. Paul F. Lazarsfeld and others of an upstate New York town.

portion for Truman as did this union. The average for six of the "poor" wards was 72.9 per cent for Truman, and for St. Louis City as a whole was 64.2 per cent.[11] Since Truman was the candidate favored by the union's leaders (as well as by most other union leaders in the country), his support from the members is an evidence partly of the success of union political education.[12]

A series of other questions was asked to find out just what the union members felt should be the role of the union in politics. In general, there seems to be strong support for the type of political action engaged in by the unions now, but less support for stronger political action (Table 22). Most members are willing to have the union leaders tell them which candidates are friendly to labor. But the union leaders have to use language carefully in doing this, as most members do not want to be "advised" how to vote.

The discrepancy between the proportion of workers who wish to be "advised" on how to vote and the proportion who simply wish to be told which candidates are friendly to labor has another important implication. It suggests that the workers will not necessarily accept any candidate, regardless of his merits and general reputation, whom the labor leaders support. Workers say they will listen to the political infor-

[11] Of course, many of the people living in these wards are members of other unions, and their pro-Truman sentiment is probably partly a result of political education in the other unions. Thus the discrepancy in the Truman vote between this union and the "poor" wards would be an insufficient measure of this union's influence.

The proportions Democratic of all votes for president in St. Louis ranged from 67.2 per cent to 79.0 per cent. The unweighted average for the six wards was 72.9 per cent. (Figures furnished through the courtesy of Dr. David Salmon.)

[12] A more recent indication of the success of the union in influencing its members politically was provided by the election in 1950 of United States Senator Thomas Hennings of Missouri. Despite the opposition of powerful Democratic forces in the primary, Hennings won the Democratic nomination for senator; and despite the drift of most of the rest of the country away from the Democratic party in that year, Hennings beat the Republican incumbent. Teamsters Local 688 was proud of the fact that Hennings made his first campaign speech to its Shop Conference, and its vigor in campaigning for Hennings undoubtedly influenced not only the membership but many other low-income people.

TABLE 22. TYPES OF POLITICAL ACTION FAVORED BY UNION MEMBERS

Question	Percentage of Members				
	Saying "Yes"	Saying "No"	Saying "Don't know"	Giving No Answer	Total *
"Should the union engage in politics in any of the following ways:					
"tell members which candidates are friendly to labor ..	77.3	20.4	...	2.3	100.0
"advise members how to vote..	35.0	62.2	...	2.8	100.0
"help to start a Labor party sometime in the future	44.9	44.4	1.3	9.4	100.0
"get union members to run for political office	69.1	25.3	...	5.6	100.0
"encourage union members to go to the polls	92.1	5.1	...	2.8	100.0
"collect a dollar from each union member to help friendly candidates	53.7	40.6	...	5.7	100.0
"spend union funds to get laws friendly to labor?"....	71.7	23.5	0.2	4.6	100.0

* The number of cases in each total is 392 – the total sample.

mation provided by their union leaders, but they do not say they will always follow their advice. As in other matters, workers distinguish their obligations and loyalty to their union from their other obligations and loyalties.

Members are overwhelmingly in favor of union leaders' encouraging them to go to the polls, which suggests that the high figure on their turnout in the 1948 election is a fairly reliable one. In answers to these questions again we see that most members favor spending regular union funds for political action (to get laws friendly to labor), but only a bare majority feel they should be assessed a dollar to help elect friendly candidates. Over two thirds of the members favor the union's encouraging its members to run for political office. This union did get one of its rank-and-filers to run for the Missouri state senate in 1948, and he was elected. When political action comes to the question of starting a labor party sometime in the future, the members are divided about half and half. Without political education to introduce it, starting a labor party would probably be a failure at this time.

E. Change in Affiliation from CIO to AF of L

Thus far in this chapter we have considered those aspects of the education of union members with which most union leaders are in agreement. In this section we consider the union members' attitudes toward a policy which was almost unique to this local union. As mentioned in Chapter I, this union was until January 1948 a member of the United Retail, Wholesale, and Department Store Employees of America, CIO. After it broke away from this international, it was an independent local known as the United Distribution Workers, affiliated locally, but not nationally, with the CIO. In February 1949 it joined the International Brotherhood of Teamsters, Chauffeurs, Warehousemen and Helpers of America, AF of L. We are not here concerned with the actual reasons for these changes, but with the members' attitudes toward and beliefs regarding the changes.

The first question asked the members to state their preference between the CIO and the AF of L affiliation, as indicated in Table 23. The distribution of answers for the total membership shows that insofar as there are any preferences between the two great labor organizations, the AF of L is preferred by a wide margin. The majority, however, seem to feel that it does not make any difference which international organization the local is affiliated with, provided the local union is good. There are no significant differences among members with different lengths of membership regarding preference for the CIO. But the older members are less inclined to prefer the AF of L and more inclined to say that international affiliation doesn't make any difference. The shop stewards are the strongest supporters of the AF of L affiliation, although still only half of them are willing to say that it is "better to be in the AF of L."

The attitudes on this issue would depend on why the union members believe there was a break with the Retail

TABLE 23. PREFERENCES OF UNION MEMBERS FOR CIO OR AF OF L AFFILIATION

	Distribution of Answers by Percentage					
			Of Nonstewards, Grouped by Years in Union			
Answer	Of All Members	Of Shop Stewards	Less than 1	1–3	4–10	Over 10
Question: "Do you think it would have been better to have remained a CIO union, or is it better to have become an AF of L union, or doesn't it make any difference providing you have a good local union?"						
"Better to have stayed in CIO"	2.6	3.2	4.6	1.4	1.7	...
"Better to be in AF of L"	36.5	49.2	40.9	36.5	32.0	19.3
"Doesn't make any difference provided the local union is good"	50.0	44.4	36.4	51.3	54.1	71.0
"Don't know"	8.7	1.6	13.6	9.5	11.6	9.7
No answer	2.2	1.6	4.5	1.3	0.6	...
Total	100.0	100.0	100.0	100.0	100.0	100.0
Number	392	64	44	74	172	31

and Wholesale Employees and why they think the union joined the Teamsters.

Table 24 shows the answers on these two questions. In reading these answers it should be understood that the members are more likely to be thinking of the specific international unions they have been members of when in the CIO and the AF of L than of the parent bodies themselves. The answers would indicate that about half the members say they have no idea why the Local broke away from the Retail and Wholesale Employees, and about 40 per cent similarly cannot express a reason why the Local joined the Teamsters. The "Don't know" answers are fewer among the older members than among the newer ones, but they form a considerable proportion for both groups. Those who do give answers give satisfactory and accurate, although incomplete, ones from the standpoint of the union leaders. There is one exception: 8.4 per cent of the members say that the Local broke away from the CIO because of personality clashes

TABLE 24. UNION MEMBERS' BELIEFS REGARDING REASONS FOR SHIFT FROM CIO TO AF OF L

Reasons Given	Percentage of Members *
Question: "Why do you think your local union broke from the Retail and Wholesale Workers Union, CIO, in the first place a little over a year ago?"	
"Misuse of Local's funds by the International" (or "Dishonest officials in International")	12.7
"Local's dissatisfaction or trouble with the International"	10.9
"Personality conflict between officers of Local and International"	8.4
"Communist influence in the International"	6.4
"AF of L is better"	4.1
"Unsatisfactory recognition of Local by International"	2.3
Miscellaneous	4.3
"Don't know"	48.0
No answer	6.4
Question: "Why do you think your local union joined the Teamsters Union, AF of L, a few months ago?"	
"Local needs the protection and support of some International"	32.4
"AF of L International is better than CIO International"	20.2
"Pressure on Local from the Teamsters International"	2.8
"Dissatisfaction with the CIO International"	1.0
Miscellaneous	3.3
"Don't know"	36.0
No answer	5.4

* The percentages total more than 100 since more than one reason could be given.

between the leaders of the Local and those of the International, and this could not be regarded as favorable to the union leaders. This reason is given much more frequently by the members who have been in the union a long time: 19.4 per cent of the members in the union ten years or more refer to personality clashes as compared to none of the new members. All the other reasons given support the policy of the Local's leaders.

In summary, there is practically no opposition from the rank and file regarding the shift from a CIO to an AF of L affiliation. The members are far from well informed, however, as to the reasons for the shift, and the matter represents a case of inadequate communication between the leaders and the rank and file.

F. Attitudes toward Union Dues and Assessments and the Disposal of Funds

We have already seen that when it comes to contributing money, the union members hesitate in their general support of the policies of the union. This is quite understandable in view of the fact that most of the members are unskilled or semiskilled workers who earn less than $50 a week. Union dues are fixed at $3 a month, which means that from 1 to 2.5 per cent (for most members closer to 2 per cent) of the wages goes for union dues. The belief that union dues are too high was expressed by 29.1 per cent of the members; 67.9 per cent said they are about right; none said they are too low (the remainder have no opinion). Older members are slightly more critical of the amount of union dues than are newer members.

In addition to dues the members are very occasionally required to pay an extra assessment to build up a strike fund, or they are strongly urged to contribute voluntarily a dollar for political action. Also, in the case of one recent prolonged strike, members were asked to contribute canned goods for the families of the strikers. Almost 90 per cent of the members do not feel that the union has asked for too many of these assessments and other extras; only 8.2 per cent explicitly say there are too many. Again it is the older members, this time including the shop stewards, who object that there are too many assessments and other extras. Those objecting include 12.9 per cent of the members who have been in the union ten years, 10.9 per cent of the shop stewards, but only 4.5 per cent of the members who have been in the union less than one year.

Another means by which the union takes money away from the members is to fine them for nonattendance at meetings. This was not done for a year or so following the passage of the Taft-Hartley Act because the practice was believed to be illegal under the Act, but a court ruling decided that such fines were simply another type of organizational commitment and therefore legal. Thus, since this survey was completed, the union has fined each member $3 for each meeting missed without a legitimate excuse.[13] Since the survey was conducted while the fine system was not in operation, the answers must be read in that context. Among the members 64.5 per cent believe that unexcused absences from meetings should be fined; 28.6 per cent are against the fines; and the remaining 6.9 per cent don't know or give no answer. The older members support the fine system just as much as do the newer members, though not so much as do the shop stewards (among whom 82.8 per cent are in favor of fines for unexcused absences).

The chief expenditures of the union are for the salaries of its staff, including the union's director.[14] The staff consists of people who do contract negotiation, shop organization, processing of grievances at the higher level, strike organization, case arguing, publicity, research, and administrative and clerical work. In connection with the union members' payments to the union treasury, their attitudes toward the salaries of the staff members would be most crucial. Apparently there is very little criticism on this score, as Table 25 shows. Only 4.6 per cent say the staff members are overpaid. A slightly larger number say they are underpaid—6.4 per cent—and half the members (49.2 per cent) say they are paid just the right amount. But it is also significant that 31.4 per cent say they don't know, and another 8.4 per cent are in this category with no answer. The table, of course, shows that those who think they pay too much dues are the ones most likely to think staff salaries are too high. What is of greater interest is that those who say they don't know about

[13] The legitimacy of the excuse is determined by the shop steward, and a very liberal interpretation is given to the rule so that the number of fines is very small.

[14] Other expenditures are for hiring meeting halls, supporting strikes, paying rent for the union's headquarters, printing and distributing a semimonthly newspaper and other publicity, paying for court costs, and so on. Formerly the union's lawyer was on the staff, but more recently an outside law firm has been hired on a retainer basis.

TABLE 25. ATTITUDES OF UNION MEMBERS REGARDING PAYMENT TO STAFF AND PAYMENT OF DUES

Answer	Distribution of Answers by Percentage		
	Of All Members	Of Members Who Think Union Dues Are: "Too high"	"About right"
Question: "Do you think the union staff members are underpaid, overpaid, or paid just right?"			
"Underpaid"	6.4	2.6 *	8.4
"Overpaid"	4.6	11.3	1.9 *
"Paid just right"	49.2	43.5	52.5
"Don't know"	31.4	33.9	28.5
No answer †	8.4	8.7	8.7
Total	100.0	100.0	100.0
Number	392	114	266

* This figure represents either (1) inconsistency or (2) misunderstanding of the questions (the question about payment to staff members may be difficult to understand), but it is too low to be concerned about.

† The constituent figures for "No answer" are higher than the total figure for "No answer" because they do not include those who had no opinion about union dues (all of whom gave answers to the question about staff salaries).

staff salaries are most likely to be the ones who say that union dues are too high. In other words, ignorance makes another slight contribution to criticism of the union.

Expenditures might be criticized on the ground not only that staff members get high salaries but also that there are too many staff members. Actually, there is little criticism on this score either. Only 5.9 per cent of the members say there are too many on the union staff, and almost as large a proportion (4.3 per cent) say there are too few. The majority (70.2 per cent) say there are about the right number. However, 19.6 per cent indicate that they do not know enough about the situation to form a judgment, and this would suggest another weakness of communication between the leaders and the rank and file.

In general, the union leaders seem to have done a good job of convincing the members that dues, extra assessments, fines for nonattendance, and staff salaries are what they should be. This is no minor achievement, since the union members have little money and are more inclined to be balky about spending it than about almost anything else connected with the union. What criticism does arise on the financial side seems to stem (1) from remembrance of earlier days when dues and assessments were lower and (2) from ignorance as to expenses.

G. Attitudes regarding Extra Services of the Union

Teamsters Local 688 seeks to provide services to its members beyond the strict trade union functions of getting higher wages, shorter hours, and better work conditions. The best example is the organization of the Labor Health Institute (LHI), through which members are given complete medical care at no cost to themselves. This is paid for by the employers, and is secured by the union in regular contract negotiations. Not all the union members belong to the LHI since collective bargaining has not been able to secure LHI services for workers in all shops.

Some of the best doctors in St. Louis are on the LHI staff (mostly part-time) and both the doctors and the equipment, as well as the organizational setup have received high praise in a report by two independent investigators.[15] Members who have had experience with the LHI are inclined to approve of it. When asked, "How does the medical service given by the Labor Health Institute compare to that given by a private doctor?" 25.8 per cent of the members said it was better, 42.9 per cent said it was about the same, 6.9 per cent said it was worse, and 24.4 per cent said they did not know or gave no answer (the latter have had no experience with the LHI). In response to another question, indicated in Table 26, 76.3 per cent think it is a very important union service to get free medical and health aid for its members

[15] Henry G. Farish, M.D., and Franz Goldman, M.D., "The Labor Health Institute: Quality of Service" (mimeographed report, 1949). The two doctors are, respectively, Specialist in Medical Audits and Hospital Consulting, Southampton, New York, and Associate Professor of Medical Care, Harvard School of Public Health, Boston, Massachusetts. The study was sponsored by the Social Planning Council of St. Louis and the Labor Health Institute.

TABLE 26. ATTITUDES OF UNION MEMBERS TOWARD EXTRA SERVICES

Answer	Percentage Giving Indicated Answer to Question: "Do you think it is important for the union to have the following services for its members even if some of the cost must come out of the union treasury?"			
	Free Legal Service	Free Medical and Health Service	Credit Union	Free Employment Service
"Yes, very important"	50.5	76.3	52.0	70.9
"Good idea, but not important"	38.0	16.8	32.9	22.5
"No, not important at all"	7.9	4.6	10.2	3.6
"Don't know"	1.3	.3	2.6	1.0
No answer	2.3	2.0	2.3	2.0
Total	100.0	100.0	100.0	100.0
Number	392	392	392	392

(and another 16.8 per cent say it is a good idea but it is not important).

Other extra services maintained by the union are free legal advice and credit unions. A majority of the members strongly endorse these too, but not in such a great proportion as in the case of the LHI. Table 26 also shows that a free employment service would be even more popular than these things, but the union does not provide that now. Not shown in the table are data indicating that those who think that union dues are too high are the ones inclined to think that these services are not quite so important. Still, their approval is only a few percentage points below that of those members who think the amount of union dues is satisfactory.

At the present time the union's office and the LHI office are located in rented quarters. Sixty-three per cent of the members say they would be in favor of the union's owning its own headquarters and having recreational facilities. This is one of the aims of the union leaders. The newer members and the shop stewards are somewhat more in favor of this proposal than are the older members.

Another existing service of the union is the publication, twice a month, of a four-page newspaper, called the *Midwest Labor World.* It is a major means of communication between the union and the members. However, only 58.7 per cent say they read every issue. Another 13.8 per cent say they read it once a month (every other issue), and the remaining 27.5 per cent read it less frequently than that. One reason for not reading the newspaper was turned up in the course of this survey: about 20 per cent of the addresses in the union's file are obsolete. The members, especially those not married, change their residence once in a while, and a certain amount of failure to keep up is natural. But 20 per cent seems a bit high and represents a significant failure in communication. It would seem that something as simple as the failure to keep up with new and correct addresses is the major cause of the members' not reading the union newspaper.

The members were asked what parts of the newspaper they usually read. The answers, by percentage of readers, were:

Headline story	71.7	Stein Shift	43.6
Front-page news	71.9	Labor Health Bulletin	60.5
Editorials	60.7	Back-page news	49.5
News from the Shops	80.4	Advertisements	19.1

The most popular feature, as these figures indicate, is "News from the Shops" (on page 3), and next in rank comes the front-page general union news. The Stein Shift (a gossip column) is the least popular feature. The newspaper would seem to be well read, according to these figures.[16]

In summary, it would appear that the union gets a good deal of membership support for its extra services – medical, legal, and credit – and for its projected services – employment agency and recreation. The newspaper is apparently liked for most of its features, especially the "News from the

[16] Figures on the parts of the paper that, in the answers to another question, the members indicated they skipped are close complements to these and hence suggest they have a high degree of reliability. The one exception is for advertisements: 55 per cent said they skipped them, but only 19.1 per cent said they read them.

Shops" and the general union news on the front page; but the newspaper fails to reach about a fifth of the members.

H. Attitudes toward Workers' Education

The modern notion of educational courses for workers dates back to the period before the First World War. While a few unions have developed it and the top union leaders give verbal sanction to it, it has never developed into a popular movement. Only a small minority of workers have taken educational courses through their unions. Nevertheless, a small group of people in the unions, or indirectly connected with unions, have worked long and hard to expand workers' education.[17] Their philosophy is that education will greatly increase the abilities of workers and thus make the union movement broader and more successful. They point out that many of the new union leaders after 1936 had taken many workers' education courses during the 1920's and early 1930's.

The philosophy of the workers' education movement has been adopted by the leaders of Teamsters Local 688, and our interest in the survey was to find out to what extent the rank and file has accepted it. Several classes for the union members are held fairly regularly, there are special educational features in the regular meetings, and the newspaper occasionally carries educational articles.

Only 6.1 per cent of the members have ever taken an educational course through the union. This proportion consists of 1.5 per cent who have taken one course, 2.3 per cent who have taken two or three courses, 0.3 per cent (that is, three tenths of 1 per cent) who have taken more than three courses, and 2.0 per cent who do not specify the number of courses taken. In other words, up to the present the classes have been concentrated on a very small proportion of the members. When the members were asked, "Would you like

[17] See Caroline B. Rose, "Workers' Education, the Labor Movement, and the Intellectuals in the United States: 1920–1940" (unpublished master's thesis, University of Chicago, 1943).

to take an education course now?" 9.2 per cent answered "Yes." If we translate this proportion into numbers for the shops covered in the survey, it would mean that 397 persons would be interested in a course. (If the figure is applied to the total membership of 8,500 – a questionable practice since the members of shops joining the union recently are less enthusiastic about union policy – we would then expect a total class attendance of 782 persons.) Another 22.2 per cent answered the question about whether they would like to take a course by saying, "Maybe later on," but this vague kind of answer usually indicates little about the respondent's real intentions. It does, however, indicate that a significant proportion of the members are open to persuasion about taking courses and are in favor of the principle of workers' education.

The members were also asked what kinds of courses they wanted, since the turnout depends on the popularity of course offerings. There were 82 spontaneous answers, which would be less than one answer apiece from each of those who say they would like to take a course either now or later on. Of the 82 answers, 37 were for a course on some aspect of union work or labor history, 27 were for a course on public speaking or "leadership" (or "how to handle people"), 9 were for a course on some technical, vocational subject (impossible for this union to give because of the variety of courses that would be needed), 3 each were for courses on politics and English composition, and 1 each for courses on religion, art, and mental hygiene.

In addition to allowing for these spontaneous answers, the schedule permitted the members to indicate a preference for suggested courses. The courses and answers are shown in Table 27. Of the four courses offered on the schedule, the most popular would be a course on labor economics and collective bargaining, and the least popular would be a course on minority groups. Even for the least popular course there is a substantial amount of interest expressed, although the absolute figures represent more of wishful thinking than of

TABLE 27. PREFERENCES OF UNION MEMBERS FOR SPECIFIED EDUCATIONAL COURSES

Answer	Percentage Giving Indicated Answer to Question: "Suppose your union offered a course on ——, would you take it?" "On present-day politics"	"On labor economics and collective bargaining"	"On public speaking"	"On minority groups such as Negroes and Jews"
"Yes"	19.1	29.6	21.4	15.9
"No"	77.3	66.6	76.0	80.2
"Don't know"; no answer	3.6	3.8	2.6	3.9
Total	100.0	100.0	100.0	100.0
Number	392	392	392	392

realistic planning. The ratio of the 9 per cent saying "Yes" to the 22 per cent saying "Maybe later on" in answer to the question on willingness to take a course should be remembered when examining the figures in Table 27.

The workers' education movement sponsors special short summer courses for workers at various points in the country, and a question was asked in the survey to get at the attitudes of the union members toward participating in one of these. The question was, "Would you be willing to attend workers' classes outside the city for 3 days to 2 weeks in the summer—like the schools at Madison and Montebello?" The percentage distribution of answers is as follows:

"Yes, very much"	8.9
"Yes, might consider it"	12.2
"No, not interested"	68.4
"Don't know"	9.7
No answer	0.8
Total	100.0

Again we see a proportion of about 9 per cent very much interested in workers' education, and another proportion—this time 12.2 per cent—amenable to it. Two thirds of the members again express no interest in it.

Still another type of workers' education is that which goes on in the regular meetings. It is used to fill up a meeting when the ordinary business of the meeting is very brief, as happens quite frequently. Since the business is usually so brief, since union leaders feel that something more than union business is necessary to promote group solidarity, and since the majority of the members do not mind filling out an hour or two once they have come together anyway, some sort of "filler" is natural. Two questions were asked on the survey to determine the members' preferences regarding the nature of the "filler." The natural alternative to an educational program of some sort is a purely social program, and the first question therefore poses the two alternatives. Table 28 shows that many more of the members prefer educational programs than prefer social affairs (32.2 to 17.6 per cent). Since a fourth of the membership would like to have both,

TABLE 28. ATTITUDES OF UNION MEMBERS TOWARD EDUCATION AS A "FILLER" AT UNION MEETINGS

Answer		Percentage of Members
Question: "Should your union have more parties and other social affairs or should there be more educational programs?"		
"More social affairs"		17.6
"More educational programs"		32.2
"More of both"		25.0
"Neither"		18.1
"Don't know"; no answer		7.1
Total		100.0
Number		392
Question: "In addition to having regular business taken up at the union meetings, would you like to have discussion, outside speakers, labor and political movies, or singing?" (If "yes," ask which.)		
"Nothing extra"		42.6 *
"Discussions"		32.7
"Outside speakers"		30.6
"Labor and political movies"		17.4
"Singing"		10.2
Others (not listed)		4.7
"Parties, dances"	2.8	
"Entertainment"	0.8	
"Prayers"	0.3	
Miscellaneous	0.8	
"Don't know"; no answer		3.1

* Percentages in answer to this second question total more than 100 since a person might give more than one answer.

it can be said that 57.2 per cent of the members are in favor of educational programs. The type of educational programs they have in mind is suggested by answers to the second question. Practically a third of the members favor discussion, only a slightly lower percentage favor outside speakers, and 17.4 per cent would like to see short movies on labor and political subjects.[18]

There are some suggestive variations in the types of persons interested in educational courses and programs. The more educated members of the union are more likely to express interest in taking educational courses than the less educated: 12.2 per cent of all those who have graduated from high school (some of whom have had a little college training) say they would like to take an educational course now, as compared to 7.6 per cent of those who have had only elementary school training. However, the more educated have not *already taken* more courses than the less educated, which may suggest that a broader program would attract more students. The list of courses spontaneously mentioned, as indicated a few pages back, suggests what offerings might attract students.

New members say they are much more interested in taking courses than older members, although shop stewards, who are likely to have been members for a long time, also want certain courses. The most popular course, labor economics and collective bargaining, for example, attracts 50 per cent of those who have been in the union less than one year, 56.2 per cent of the shop stewards, but only 12.9 per cent of those who have been members more than ten years. Similar differences appear for the other specific courses listed (see Table 27). The difference does not occur, however, for the summer course offered out of town for from three days to two weeks. Only the shop stewards stand out at all in desir-

[18] "Singing" was put into the printed list for the sake of comparison. It attracted less interest than the three kinds of educational programs listed. Social affairs and entertainment were mentioned spontaneously by small proportions, but the proportions would have been considerably larger if these activities had been specifically listed.

ing this course, with 17.2 per cent saying that they would very much like to take it.

When it comes to educational programs in the regular union meetings, there is an interesting difference in the answers. Older members favor educational programs significantly more than do newer members (38.7 per cent of those with over ten years' membership as compared to 25.0 per cent of those with less than one year's membership), and shop stewards are most in favor, with 43.8 per cent. Older members are least in favor of social affairs (9.7 per cent of the older group in favor as compared to 20.5 per cent of the newest group and 12.5 per cent among shop stewards). When it comes to specifying precisely what they would prefer, however, the older members are somewhat more inclined to say they would prefer nothing in addition to business at the regular meetings (54.8 per cent among the oldest members in favor of nothing extra as compared to 43.2 per cent among the newest). Otherwise there is not much difference by length of membership in favor of such specific items as discussions, outside speakers, and labor and political movies.

In summary, only about 9 per cent of the members are convinced that they should take educational courses,[19] but a slight majority are in favor of educational programs as part of the regular union meetings. The more educated members and the newer members are more willing to take courses. But the older members are slightly more in favor of educational programs as compared to social affairs as fillers for the regular meetings, although they would prefer nothing extra at all. Courses dealing with the economics of labor and the problems of unionism are most popular among the special courses. For regular meetings, educational discussions and outside speakers are the most popular fillers.

It is impossible to say from the data presented in this section whether or not the union has had any effect in encour-

[19] It should be understood that when the union members speak of education, they are thinking of education as offered by the workers' education movement rather than education as offered by colleges or secondary schools.

aging an open attitude toward workers' education. Certainly the bulk of the members have no great enthusiasm for workers' education, and it may be that those who do have would have been in the same proportion if the union did not push it. There is, however, a nucleus of interest, and it can probably be expanded by further efforts.

I. Summary

1. The members are about equally divided regarding incentive pay (as compared to weekly wages fixed according to the job). The union leaders seem to have had some effect in encouraging this attitude.

2. Three fourths of the members say they favor strict application of the seniority principle in promotions and layoffs, and some 15 per cent more favor a modified seniority system. This strong support has undoubtedly been achieved in part through the work of the union leaders.

3. Only a small proportion of the members are against the union's engaging in further organizational work. But there is a limit to the time and money they feel should be spent on new organization. Roughly equal thirds of the members say they would have the union concentrate primarily on organization, on improving conditions for the existing members, and on dividing the money and effort equally between these two. Four fifths of the members are willing to help picket a shop other than their own to aid a strike or help promote a new organizational drive. It would seem that the union has been very successful in getting its membership to support new organizational work.

4. The union members support political action overwhelmingly if it involves simply being encouraged to go to the polls, being told which candidates are prolabor, and helping to get prolabor legislation passed. They are against being told whom to vote for. They are divided about equally regarding having a Labor party at this time. Only a bare majority are in favor of an extra assessment for political action, even if it is only $1 during election years, but most are

willing to have regular union funds spent for political action. The general support for political action seems to be another evidence of success on the part of the union leaders.

5. Most members are indifferent toward the shift from a CIO international affiliation to an AF of L international affiliation, and about half have no understanding of the reasons for the shift. Only 2.6 per cent say it would have been better to remain in the CIO, and only 8.4 per cent attribute the break with the CIO to such an unflattering cause as a personality conflict between leaders of the international and local unions. While the members support the union leaders on the shift, there is evidence that the leaders did a weak job of communicating to the rank and file the nature of the move and the reasons for it.

6. While the majority of the members feel that union dues are just about right, 29.1 per cent feel they are too high. A like proportion is against fines for nonattendance at meetings. There is practically no criticism of extra assessments to date. There is practically no criticism of the salaries of staff members.

7. Most of the members who have had experience with the medical services of the Labor Health Institute, through which the union gets free medical care for most of its members (paid for by the employers), are enthusiastic about them. The members are also in favor of the legal service, the credit union, and the newspaper, but are more strongly in favor of two extra services which the union does not now provide—a free employment service and recreational facilities. The chief difficulty with the newspaper seems to be that a significant minority do not receive it. The most popular features in the newspaper are the "News from the Shops" and the general news on the front page.

8. Only a small proportion of the members are interested in educational courses given through the union, and a bare majority are in favor of educational programs given as part of the regular union meetings. Since it is the newer members who are most interested in the courses, and since the older

members prefer the educational programs only as an alternative to social affairs, it cannot be said that the union leaders have been successful in convincing the members that workers' education is an important thing for them. There is some evidence that greater effort will have some effect on a minority of the members.

CHAPTER V

The Members' Attitudes toward Minority Groups

A. Introduction: The Union Opposes the Dominant Culture Pattern

One of the policies of the union leadership in Teamsters Local 688 is to promote racial and religious equality among its members and, to a lesser extent, in the St. Louis area.[1] Activities in behalf of ethnic equality occur not only in the economic sphere, but in the legal and social spheres as well. For example, the union occasionally sponsors mixed social affairs; it has been very influential in opening the recreational facilities of the city's largest park to Negroes; it has been one of the sponsors of a petition to the city council in favor of a Civil Rights Ordinance for St. Louis.

In the shops the union tried to get qualified Negroes up-

[1] Other studies of integrating Negroes and whites by means of unions include: (1) Calvin Wayne Gordon, "Techniques for the Integration of Negroes in Industry through Labor Unions" (unpublished master's thesis, Department of Sociology, Washington University, June 1945); (2) Ira N. Brophy, "The Luxury of Anti-Negro Prejudice," *Public Opinion Quarterly*, IX (Winter 1945–1946), 456–466; (3) Georgia Workers Education Service, *Our First Year* (Atlanta, 1947); (4) Frank Winn, "Labor Tackles the Race Question," *Antioch Review*, III (Fall 1943), 341–360. In 1949 the United Packinghouse Workers of America, CIO, conducted a formal self-study of group relations. Other studies of integrating racial groups in industry include various reports on the success of federal and state F.E.P.C.'s; studies referred to in Arnold Rose, *Studies in Reduction of Prejudice* (Chicago: American Council on Race Relations, 1948), especially p. 14; and studies reported in various issues of the *Inventory of Research in Racial and Cultural Relations* (Chicago: American Council on Race Relations, 1948 and after).

graded just as whites are, and it has succeeded in getting Negro taxicab drivers into the lines at the bus and railroad terminals. The union newspaper has regularly carried pro-minority articles and news, and most of the members have been made aware of the leaders' attitude on minority issues through speeches, personal contacts, and so on. During the year preceding the survey the union had the collaboration of the St. Louis Labor Education Project, which, operating on funds from outside sources, has been primarily promoting education for better intergroup relations.

The policy of the union is fairly rare in the city of St. Louis. Though St. Louis is a border city rather than a southern city and there has been practically no effort to deprive Negroes of the vote or to engage in violence against them, they have been traditionally accorded a definitely lower place in the economic and social scale. Only a few firms hire Negroes in better-grade jobs, and only four or five of the unions in addition to Teamsters Local 688 avoid segregating them in one way or another. Even some of the other local unions in the city whose international affiliations are militantly equalitarian are themselves engaged in practicing segregation in local union organization or in social affairs, and none does much about getting equal rights for Negroes on the job. In several respects the unions in St. Louis are less equalitarian than are some unions in the deep South. Thus Teamsters Local 688 stands out and is known throughout the city for its relatively equalitarian policy.

One way of regarding the central problem of this chapter is to determine the extent to which nonminority members of the union have been influenced by the leaders' policy. Is the policy a success in terms of what nonminority members think of the minority, in terms of changes in their attitudes, and in terms of what they think of the leaders' efforts in behalf of equal treatment for minorities?

Another way of regarding the central problem of this chapter is to put it into the context of union solidarity, which is the theme of the whole study. There are Negro, Jewish, and Catholic members of the union, and potentially members of any of these or other minorities could join in even greater numbers. The question becomes, Does union solidarity encompass these minorities, which the general culture of the United States singles out for prejudice and discrimination? To what extent do union members express the general prejudices of our culture, and to what extent solidarity with all union members?

The questions asked on the survey relate primarily to Negroes and Jews, although one question was asked about Catholics, and a few were asked about minorities in general.[2] Jews constitute less than 1.3 per cent of the membership, as indicated by the sample survey, and thus could not significantly affect the answers to be reported in this chapter. Negroes constitute 4.9 per cent of the sample surveyed, and therefore were eliminated from the tabulation of all questions about Negroes and about minorities in general.[3]

Since Jews form such a small proportion of the total membership of the union, they could not be regarded as much of an internal union problem. There is a Jew on the union staff, however, who occupies the important position of chief organizer, and attitudes toward him are the major way in which attitudes toward Jews on the part of the rank and file might affect the union directly. Negroes not only constitute a large proportion of the sample surveyed, but there are some shops in the union that were not surveyed[4] which are predominantly or exclusively Negro in membership. Thus Negroes are present at all union meetings and at stewards' meetings in significant numbers. Catholics who say they attend church constitute 34.5 per cent of the membership, and

[2] Many of the questions on ethnic attitudes used in the survey and reported on in this chapter were originally formulated by the Department of Scientific Research of the American Jewish Committee, under the direction of Dr. Samuel Flowerman, or by the Bureau of Applied Social Research of Columbia University, under the direction of Dr. Paul F. Lazarsfeld.

[3] As a matter of fact, Negroes were not asked these questions, although they were asked questions about Jews and Catholics, and their answers are included in tables referring to the latter minority groups.

[4] Because they joined the union more recently than seven years before the survey.

are thus a most significant element within the union. White Protestant church attenders form 33.8 per cent of the membership. Another 18.1 per cent consists of nonchurchgoers who admit a Protestant or Catholic background (predominantly Protestant), 3.8 per cent refuse to indicate church preference or background, and for the remaining 3.6 per cent we have no information.

B. Economic Attitudes toward Negroes

Attitudes toward Negroes on the part of white union members form a complicated pattern. Answers differ decidedly, depending on whether the question refers to Negroes in an economic situation, a social situation, or a specifically union situation. We shall consider attitudes in these three types of situations in turn.

There are two major kinds of economic problems for Negroes toward which the white union members can be expected to have definite attitudes: getting a job and getting promoted ("upgraded") on the job. A question was asked in the survey on each of these matters, and the answers are indicated in Table 29. It will be seen that many more white union members are against the union's seeking economic equality for Negroes than are for it. Still, if those who are in favor of the union's seeking a measure of economic justice for Negroes be added to those who favor more active efforts, the two groups constitute a bare majority. It can therefore be said that the white union members are fairly equally split regarding whether the union should seek jobs and promotions for Negroes.

Unwillingness to have the union help Negroes get jobs when there are vacancies in the shops where the white union members work is due almost entirely to personal antipathy toward Negroes and not due to a belief that this is not particularly a union function or a belief that it might be bad for Negroes. This is shown by the fact that 87 per cent of those who think it is a bad idea for the union to help Negroes also express a personal antipathy against working side by side

TABLE 29. ATTITUDES OF WHITE UNION MEMBERS TOWARD THE ECONOMIC POSITION OF NEGROES

	Percentage Giving Indicated Answer to Question:	
Answer	"Do you think it is a good idea or a bad idea for your union to try to get Negroes into jobs in the place where you work, when there are vacancies?"	"Do you think it is a good idea or a bad idea for your union to try to get Negroes into all kinds of jobs in the place, including good jobs, when there are vacancies and Negroes have seniority?"
"Good idea"	16.6	20.9
"Bad idea"	44.2	47.5
"O.K. up to a point"	37.0	28.4
"Don't know"; no answer	2.2	3.2
Total	100.0	100.0
Number	373	373

with Negroes, as compared to only 19 per cent expressing this personal antipathy among those who think it is a good idea for the union to help Negroes.

Catholics among the members are more likely to be in favor of the union's seeking economic equality for Negroes than are Protestants, although nonchurchgoers of either Catholic or Protestant background are most in favor by a significant proportion (Table 30). This might be explainable in terms of the more explicitly equalitarian policy of the Catholic church in St. Louis, and of the generally greater liberalism of nonchurchgoers. The difference is not so much in the proportion of those saying the union's efforts would be a "bad idea," as it is in those who say the union's efforts are a "good idea" and "O.K. up to a point."

In the first question, on the union's getting jobs for Negroes, there was another breakdown by educational status. Table 30 shows that the high school graduates (some of whom have gone to college) are more liberal toward Negroes than are the less well educated members of the union.

Still another breakdown is by length of union member-

TABLE 30. ATTITUDES OF WHITE UNION MEMBERS TOWARD THE UNION'S GETTING JOBS FOR NEGROES, ACCORDING TO RELIGION, EDUCATION, AND LONGEVITY IN THE UNION

Category of Members	Percentage Expressing Indicated Attitude toward Jobs for Negroes					
	"Good idea"	"Bad idea"	"O.K. up to a point"	"Don't know"; No Answer	Total	Number
			Religion			
Church-attending Catholics	17.8	43.7	34.8	3.7	100.0	135
Church-attending Protestants	10.5	46.6	41.4	1.5	100.0	133
Nonchurchgoers, Catholic or Protestant	25.4	40.8	33.8	...	100.0	71
			Education			
Grammar school	17.6	50.0	30.2	2.2	100.0	182
Some high school	14.4	47.8	35.1	2.7	100.0	111
High school graduation or some college	18.7	25.0	53.8	2.5	100.0	80
			Longevity in the Union			
Members under 1 year	22.7	38.6	36.4	2.3	100.0	44
Members 1–3 years ..	11.0	38.3	50.7	...	100.0	73
Members 4–10 years ..	14.5	47.2	37.1	1.2	100.0	159
Members over 10 years	6.9	51.7	34.5	6.9	100.0	29
Shop stewards	30.6	43.6	22.6	3.2	100.0	62

ship: it shows that newer members are considerably more liberal toward Negroes than are older members. The shop stewards are divided sharply. They have the largest proportion saying that it is a good idea for the union to help Negroes to get jobs, but the proportion among them saying that it is a bad idea is almost as high as the comparable proportion among older members. On the basis of this evidence on the attitudes of the shop stewards and of the older members, it can hardly be said that the union leaders' policy of promoting economic equality for Negroes has served to educate the members. More important would seem to be the general tendency for younger people, who also tend to be the newer members, to be more liberal on racial matters.

The questions mentioned thus far were about what the *union* should do about Negroes. Two other questions were about *personal* relations with Negroes on the job and have important implications for the economic position of Negroes. The first question and the answers to it are shown in Table 31. A bare majority of the union members say they dislike

TABLE 31. ATTITUDES OF WHITE UNION MEMBERS TOWARD WORKING WITH NEGROES

	Distribution of Answers by Percentage			
		Of White Members Grouped by Attitude toward the Union's Getting Jobs for Negroes at the Member's Place of Work		
Answer	Of All White Members	"Good idea"	"O.K. up to a point"	"Bad idea"
Question: "Do you dislike working side by side with Negroes, doing the same kind of job?"				
"Yes, dislike very much"	51.2	10.9	40.9	76.1
"Dislike a little, but not seriously"	17.4	7.8	31.4	10.4
"No, don't dislike at all"	27.6	73.5	26.3	9.8
"Don't know"; no answer	3.8	7.8	1.4	3.7
Total	100.0	100.0	100.0	100.0
Number	373	64	163	137

very much working side by side with Negroes. Another 17.4 per cent say they dislike it a little, but not seriously, and over a fourth (27.6 per cent) say they don't dislike it at all.

As one would expect, there is a strong relationship between the answers to this question and the answers to the previously discussed question about whether the members think the union should help get jobs for Negroes.[5] But the relationship is not perfect. Most interesting is the fact that among those who think the union should help Negroes get jobs 10.9 per cent admit a strong personal antipathy to Negroes, 7.8 per cent say they dislike working with Negroes a

[5] The two questions were on different pages of the schedule so that there is little likelihood of simply remembering one's answer to one question and answering the second question in the light of the first.

little, and there is the large group (7.8 per cent) who "don't know" or give no answer. All these categories of people seem to be members who have been influenced by the union's equalitarian position, but who have not, or have not yet, incorporated that position into their personal feelings.

On the other hand, there are the 9.8 per cent among those who think it is a bad idea for the union to get jobs for Negroes who say they don't dislike working side by side with Negroes. These people are either rationalizing ("Some of my good friends are Negroes, but . . .") or they have conflicting motivations and attitudes with respect to Negroes. They should be more intensively studied, through a prolonged interview, but in this study there were no facilities for doing so. It is also obvious from the answers indicated in Table 31 that the group which believes that it is "O.K. up to a certain point" for the union to get Negroes into jobs is the one currently most amenable to change in either direction: 40.9 per cent of them admit strong personal antipathy to Negroes, but 26.3 per cent say they have no personal antipathy at all.

The final measure of attitudes regarding personal relations with Negroes on the job is based on responses to the statement that "Negroes should be put on separate jobs from whites." The figures corroborate those of Table 31. Slightly over a fourth of the members are definitely against job segregation of Negroes; almost three fifths are in favor of it; and the remaining 14.2 per cent say they can't make up their minds.

C. Social Attitudes toward Negroes

The question on job separation just mentioned has not only economic but also social implications for relations between the races. That is probably why the answers are more anti-Negro than the answers to the first two questions, which have more exclusively economic implications. More whites will be found to favor economic equality for Negroes than social equality in almost any social context in the United States.[6] In this section we shall examine questions dealing

[6] This is part of Myrdal's rank order theory of discrimination. (Gunnar

more exclusively with social relations and shall find that the union members are more decidedly anti-Negro in these respects than in economic matters.

Two of the questions dealing with social relations are concerned with the location of Negro residences (Table 32).

TABLE 32. ATTITUDES OF WHITE UNION MEMBERS AND OF THE GENERAL ST. LOUIS POPULATION TOWARD THE LOCATION OF NEGRO RESIDENCES

	Distribution of Answers by Percentage	
Answer	Of White Union Members	Of General Population of St. Louis
Question: "Do you think that Negroes should be permitted to live in the same block with white persons?"		
"Yes"	13.9	12.5
"No"	83.7	85.6
"Don't know"; no answer	2.4	1.9
Total	100.0	100.0
Number	373	
Question: "Do you think that Negroes should be permitted to live in the same building with white persons?"		
"Yes"	10.2	9.7
"No"	88.8	88.4
"Don't know"; no answer	1.0	1.9
Total	100.0	100.0
Number	373	

Not only do we have the answers to these questions from union members but also from a representative cross section of the population of St. Louis and St. Louis County.[7] It can readily be seen not only that an overwhelming proportion is against living close to Negroes, but also that the union members' attitudes do not differ significantly from those of the

Myrdal with the assistance of Richard Sterner and Arnold Rose, *An American Dilemma*, New York: Harper, 1944, pp. 60–61.) The theory as a whole applies only to southern whites, but this aspect of it applies to northern whites also.

[7] The sample for the representative cross section of the general population was drawn by the "area method." The questions were asked as part of a survey on attitudes toward housing in November 1947. The survey was under the general direction of Edward B. Olds, Hazel P. Maxwell, and Arnold M. Rose.

general population. Practically all of the union members are in the lower-income classes, whereas the general population, of course, includes all income classes. Other studies show that people of lower income have more prejudice against Negroes than do those of middle and higher incomes, and on this basis alone we might expect that the union members would be more prejudiced than the general population. Since they are not more prejudiced, the possibility is left open that their union affiliation may be a slightly liberalizing influence. Catholics in the union are again more liberal than Protestants, but just the opposite was found to be true in the general population.[8] In the union 14.8 per cent of the church-attending Catholics, as compared to 8.3 per cent of the church-attending Protestants and 19.7 per cent of the nonchurchgoers, think that Negroes should be permitted to live in the same block with white persons. And 8.9 per cent of the churchgoing Catholics, as compared to 5.3 per cent of the churchgoing Protestants and 9.9 per cent of the nonchurchgoers, think that Negroes should be permitted to live in the same building with white persons.

A significant educational difference also appears in attitudes toward having social relations with Negroes. While 21.3 per cent of those who have graduated from high school are willing to have Negroes live in the same block, only 12.1 per cent of the grammar school group and 11.7 per cent of the "some high school" group are willing.

Another difference that would be of great interest if it were larger suggests a connection between personality traits and attitudes toward having social relations with Negroes. Those who want their union to be democratically run are slightly more willing to let Negroes live in the same block with whites. But the difference is barely significant in a statistical sense (12 per cent as compared to 15 per cent) and no reliance can be placed on it.

[8] This apparent contradiction might be explained by the fact that Protestants in the general population include many more middle and upper income people than do Catholics, and middle and upper income people are generally more liberal toward Negroes than are lower income people.

It is to be expected that those who believe in economic equality for Negroes are more liberal toward Negroes on social matters also. Still, almost two thirds (65.6 per cent) of those who believe the union should help get jobs for Negroes would not have Negroes living in the same building with white persons. Of course, practically no one is in favor of social equality if he is against economic equality; so this 65.6 per cent is to be compared to the almost 100 per cent of those disapproving of the union's helping Negroes who are against living in the same building with them.

Another question regarding general social relations between whites and Negroes is, "Would you object to Negro and white children going to the same school?" Almost a fourth (24.5 per cent) of the members said they would not object, showing more liberalism in the matter of school segregation than in the matter of residential segregation. St. Louis public schools are segregated by law, but the Catholic parochial schools recently abolished segregation by order of the Archbishop. This difference is reflected again in the greater liberalness of Catholic union members as compared to Protestant union members, although nonchurchgoers are the most liberal of all.[9]

D. Attitudes toward Negroes in the Union Situation

Social relations in the union on job situations are to be distinguished, for some members, from social relations in the home or school. This is a reflection of what we have already seen, namely, that many more members are willing to be

[9] The three questions on attitudes toward Negroes being in the same block, in the same building, and in the same school formed a scale (in the Guttman sense) with a reproducibility of 99 per cent for a sample of Minneapolis residents in another study conducted by the author. But the three questions did not form a scale for our sample of union members or the general population of St. Louis. The reason is believed to be the injection of the school segregation issue into popular discussion by the Catholic church in St. Louis, so that Protestants and Catholics were reacting differently to the three questions. This illustrates a limitation to scales, and to the very concept of scaling, that Guttman refers to when there is subcultural variation in a society. (S. A. Stouffer, L. Guttman, *et al.*, *Measurement and Prediction* [Princeton: Princeton University Press, 1950].)

equalitarian in economic relations than in social ones. But when we come to a question which ties social relations to economic ones, some flexible members go one way and others go another, as we would expect. To the question, "Do you think that when the union has parties, picnics, and dances, there should be separate ones for Negroes, or should Negroes

TABLE 33. ATTITUDES OF WHITE UNION MEMBERS TOWARD NEGROES IN THE UNION SITUATION

Answer	Percentage Giving Indicated Answer to Question: "Do you think it is a good idea or a bad idea to have Negroes on a picket line along with whites?"	Percentage Giving Indicated Answer to Question: "What do you think of having Negroes on the union staff?"
"Good idea"	31.9	29.8
"Doesn't make any difference"	42.1	34.6
"Bad idea"	24.4	33.8
"Don't know"; no answer	1.6	1.8
Total	100.0	100.0
Number	373	373

be invited to the same social affairs with whites?" the white members replied as follows: 60.3 per cent favored separate affairs for Negroes; 19.6 per cent favored having Negroes and whites at the same affairs; 11.8 per cent said Negroes should be allowed to come, but not encouraged; 7.5 per cent said they didn't care either way; and the remaining 0.8 per cent did not answer. The proportion in favor of equality for Negroes on this question is larger than on other questions dealing with social relations, but smaller than on questions dealing with economic relations. The antipathy toward having social relations with Negroes seems to be modified, for some members, by a feeling that Negroes should be treated as equals in the union.[10]

[10] When asked a general question about the organization of social affairs for the union, white members forget about Negroes. Answers to the question, "What is the best way of organizing social affairs regarding who should be invited?" show that a majority (53.8 per cent) favor social affairs for "anyone in the union who wants to come." While these answers show a

Much stronger evidence that some members believe in treating Negroes as equals in the union situation comes from the answers to two other questions. Both of these questions deal with relations to Negroes in a union situation without the influence of the touchy issue of social relations. The answers to the two questions are shown in Table 33. They indicate considerably more friendliness to Negroes than was shown in any of the questions we have examined up to this point. Only 24.4 per cent of the white members feel it is a bad idea to have Negroes on a picket line, and only 33.8 per cent feel it is a bad idea to have Negroes on the union staff.[11] It would seem, therefore, that a sizable majority of the white members are completely willing to have Negroes in the same union and to give them full rights as union members except as these rights involve social relations with whites.

This leads us back to our original question regarding the success of the union policy toward Negroes. One measure of the success of the union in the eyes of the members comes from answers to the question, "In general, what do you think of the way your union is run?" The answers to this question were cross-tabulated with the answers to the one about having Negroes on the union staff, to determine the relationship between the two questions and thus get an indication of the connection between these diverse measures of solidarity. The results show that among those who most approve of the union's direction, there is a somewhat larger number who believe it a good idea to have Negroes on the staff. Of those saying the union is run very well, 32.6 per cent said it is a good idea to have Negroes on the union staff, as compared to 25.8 per cent giving this answer among those saying the

general predilection for union-wide social affairs, they are given in forgetfulness of all-Negro or dominantly Negro shops and the stated desire not to have social affairs with Negroes. Whether or not the desire for union-wide socials could be used to integrate Negroes more into the union cannot be determined from these data.

[11] At the time of the survey there were two Negroes on the union staff — one in an important organizing, shop-servicing function and the other in research. Most members probably knew of the former person, but few knew of the latter (because he was a recent appointee and because his job did not bring him into contact with many rank-and-file members).

union is run fairly well. There are too few members saying the union is not run so well, or is run poorly, to justify a tabulation for them. It would seem, then, that approval of the union's Negro policy is one factor in general satisfaction with the direction of the union. In other words, those most "sold" on the union in general have been most influenced by the leaders' equalitarian policy toward Negroes.

A final question on this subject asks directly about union policy. The question and answers, cross-tabulated by length of membership in the union, are shown in Table 34. Again

TABLE 34. ATTITUDES OF WHITE UNION MEMBERS TOWARD THE UNION POLICY REGARDING MINORITIES

	Distribution of Answers by Percentage					
			Of Nonstewards, Grouped by Years in Union			
Answer	Of All White Members	Of Shop Stewards	Less than 1	1–3	4–10	Over 10
Question: "Do you think the union spends too much time, not enough time, or about the right amount of time, on matters affecting Negroes and other minority groups?"						
"Not enough time"	6.1	9.7	4.5	5.5	5.6	3.4
"Too much time"	5.3	11.3	2.3	2.7	3.1	13.8
"About the right amount"	50.6	61.3	40.9	49.3	50.7	48.3
"Don't know" ..	36.7	16.1	52.3	42.5	39.5	34.5
No answer	1.3 *	1.6	...	...	1.1	...
Total	100.0	100.0	100.0	100.0	100.0	100.0
Number	373	62	44	73	159	29

* This percentage is larger than other percentages for "No answer" because "All White Members" includes six persons for whom we have no information regarding either longevity or shop steward status.

we see that there is very little criticism regarding union policy—in this case the union's policy of seeking more equalitarian treatment of Negroes. A large proportion (36.7 per cent) do not wish to express their opinion about the union's policy and so say, "Don't know," or else they are new members who really do not know the union's policy. Older members naturally include the lowest proportion of "Don't know" answers. They also include the largest proportion of those critical of the union's policy in saying that the union spends too much time on matters affecting Negroes. Shop stewards include the largest proportion of those saying that the union does not spend enough time on these matters, but also are next to the oldest members in the proportion saying that the union spends too much time on them. This occurs because the shop stewards have the smallest proportion unwilling or unable to give an answer to the question.

If we try to summarize the white members' attitudes toward Negroes and their relations with them, we come to the following general observations: (1) The great majority of the white members are against having social relations with Negroes. (2) They are about evenly divided in their attitudes with respect to a more nearly equal position for Negroes on jobs and promotions. (3) In the strictly union situation a considerable majority favor equal treatment of Negroes. (4) There is very little criticism of the union's policy of trying to secure more nearly equal treatment of Negroes.

These facts help to explain an apparent inconsistency in workers' behavior which has disturbed some social scientists and liberal labor leaders. They have assumed that the efforts of some unions to reduce race prejudice among their members have had no effect because the workers participate in race conflict in their home environments. In a discussion of "inconsistency" in race relations, Marie Jahoda, for example, observes: "Trade union officials in Detroit who had consistently advocated and implemented a policy of non-segregation and educated their membership to the acceptance of this principle were disturbed to learn that some of their staunchest union members had actively participated in the race riots in 1943."[12] The Detroit riot was precipitated over the issue of segregation in housing. From our study it is apparent that a union can be quite successful in educating

[12] Marie Jahoda, "Consistency and Inconsistency in Intergroup Relations," *Journal of Social Issues*, V, No. 3 (1949), 4.

its members for nondiscrimination in the work or union situation, but create no carry-over effect to the home situation.[13] This is in conformity with the general finding of social psychology that people do not feel the same way about a given social object in differing social situations.

E. Attitudes toward Jews and Catholics

There are very few Jews among the members of the union, especially in the shops we are studying (1.3 per cent in the sample surveyed). Several of the employers are Jewish, however. The union members' attitudes are conditioned by that fact, as well as by the general climate of opinion regarding Jews in American society and the union's antidiscrimination policy. Because the position of Jews is different from that of Negroes, even though both may be called minority groups, some of the questions asked about Jews on the survey are different.

Those questions that are the same for Jews as the ones already analyzed for Negroes are reported in Table 35. Apparently very few union members (3.8 per cent) have a strong personal antipathy to working side by side with a Jew, but a larger proportion (10.5 per cent) say they have a mild personal antipathy. Still, the feeling in this regard is nothing like that with respect to Negroes. Almost 40 per cent of the members are in favor of having Jews on the union staff,[14] and 50 per cent more say they have no attitude as to whether or not there is a Jew on the union staff. Still, there remain the 9.4 per cent who are against having Jews on the union staff.

It is something like this last mentioned proportion of the union's members which is out-and-out anti-Semitic. For example, on questions regarding job discrimination and resi-

[13] This conclusion has been independently arrived at in two other studies involving different unions in different cities. See Dietrich C. Reitzes, "Collective Factors in Race Relations," unpublished Ph.D. thesis, University of Chicago, 1950; and John Hope, unpublished study of the Packinghouse Workers Union of Kansas City, Fisk University, 1949.

[14] A Jew occupies the important post of chief organizer on the union staff.

TABLE 35. ATTITUDES OF UNION MEMBERS TOWARD WORKING SIDE BY SIDE WITH JEWS AND TOWARD HAVING JEWS ON THE UNION STAFF

Answer	Percentage of Members
Question: "Do you dislike working side by side with a Jew, doing the same kind of work?"	
"Yes, dislike very much"	3.8
"Dislike a little, but not seriously"	10.5
"No, don't dislike at all"	80.9
"Don't know"; no answer	4.8
Total	100.0
Number	392
Question: "What do you think of having Jews on the union staff?"	
"Good idea"	39.3
"Bad idea"	9.4
"Don't care either way"	50.0
"Don't know"; no answer	1.3
Total	100.0
Number	392

dential segregation, it is by almost the same low percentage that the union members favor these things. Table 36 shows that 6.6 per cent of the members explicitly favor keeping Jews out of jobs, and 8.4 per cent favor keeping Jews out of Christian neighborhoods. Another 23.0 per cent or 19.1 per cent, depending on which of these two questions is examined, are mild or potential anti-Semites according to their answers.

Much of the antagonism against Jews in the United States is closely associated with certain stereotypes. Among the most powerful of these is that Jews dominate business and politics. Questions on these matters have usually been found to bring out even the mild anti-Semites. The answers are also shown in Table 36. More than a fourth of the members (26.8 per cent) apparently believe that Jews have too much power in the business world already, and another 20.1 per cent can't decide. In respect to political power, the stereotype is not so strong: 14.8 per cent would prevent Jews from holding high political office, and 22.2 per cent more can't decide.

The feeling against Jews' holding high political office is

TABLE 36. AGREEMENT OR DISAGREEMENT OF UNION MEMBERS WITH STATEMENTS REGARDING JEWS

Attitude Expressed	Percentage Expressing Indicated Attitude	
	"It would be a good idea if more business concerns would refuse to hire Jews"	*"It would be a good idea to keep Jews out of Christian neighborhoods"*
"Agree"	6.6	8.4
"Disagree"	69.1	71.5
"Can't decide"	23.0	19.1
No answer	1.3	1.0
Total	100.0	100.0
Number	392	392
	"It would be a good idea if Jews were prevented from getting more power in the business world"	*"In general Jews should not be allowed to hold high political office"*
"Agree"	26.8	14.8
"Disagree"	51.5	61.2
"Can't decide"	20.1	22.2
"Don't know"; no answer	1.6	1.8
Total	100.0	100.0
Number	392	392

sometimes also expressed against Catholics. The feeling that Catholics would be dangerous if given high political office, because the government could then be run by the church, is one of the few stereotypes against Catholics. On this point, therefore, we can directly compare attitudes toward Jews and toward Catholics. Since Catholic churchgoers form a third of the union membership, while Jews form only a negligible proportion, it is necessary to report the figures separately for members with different church affiliations. Table 37 shows that the feeling against Catholics' holding high political office is concentrated among the Protestant churchgoers, although a significant minority of Catholics themselves say they "agree" or "can't decide" (2.9 plus 13.4 per cent). Again we see that the nonchurchgoers are more liberal than the Protestant churchgoers. A comparison of the figures in Tables 36 and 37 shows that the Protestants are

TABLE 37. ATTITUDES OF UNION MEMBERS TOWARD CATHOLICS' HOLDING HIGH POLITICAL OFFICE

Attitude Expressed	Distribution of Attitudes by Percentage: Of All Members *	Of White Catholic Church-goers	Of White Protestant Church-goers	Of White Nonchurch-goers of Catholic or Protestant Background
Statement: "In general, Catholics should not be allowed to hold high political office."				
"Agree"	7.6	2.9	12.0	5.6
"Disagree"	71.7	82.2	61.7	80.3
"Can't decide"	19.4	13.4	24.8	12.7
"Don't know"; no answer	1.3	1.5	1.5	1.4
Total	100.0	100.0	100.0	100.0
Number	392	135	133	71

* "All Members" includes Jews and Negroes, who are too few in numbers to report separately.

almost as much against Catholics' holding high political office as the general membership is against Jews' holding high political office. It would seem, therefore, that the lesser degree of prejudice expressed against Catholics in these questions is primarily due to the large proportion of Catholics in the union.

F. Changes in Ethnic Attitudes as a Consequence of Union Membership

We have already observed two facts which suggest that union membership has weakened prejudice against Negroes and other minorities: (1) Many more white members are willing to have equal treatment of Negroes in the union than in outside social relations or even in the job situation. (2) There is little criticism that the union spends too much time in prominority activities. We have also noted one fact which suggests that the union's policy has not reduced prejudice: The members who have been in the union for a long time are less in favor of the union's helping Negroes get jobs and promotions than are the newer members. In this section we shall consider further evidence regarding change in ethnic attitudes.

Two questions ask directly whether the member thinks his attitude has changed toward Negroes and Jews since joining the union, and, if so, in what direction. People are not always aware of changes in their attitudes, and therefore answers to this question would not be a full measure of change. On the other hand, those who say they are aware of change are likely to have actually changed, so that the proportion reported would at least be a minimum. The questions ask about change in attitude "since you became a member of the union." This does not necessarily mean that the union experiences were the only ones causing the change. There were many other happenings in the United States which might have influenced the member to change his attitude in a prominority direction. On the other hand, since the question specifically mentions the union, the member is likely to think of union experiences as the main cause of change, if any. Also, this investigator would guess that most lower-income St. Louisans were shielded from many of the social changes regarding minorities going on in other parts of the country.[15]

Table 38 gives the answers to the two questions regarding changes in attitudes toward Negroes and Jews. It shows that almost 12 per cent say they have become more friendly to Negroes, and almost 5 per cent say they have become more friendly to Jews. About 1 per cent of the members say they have become less friendly to Negroes and Jews. The increased friendliness toward Negroes is quite significant, considering the deep-seated character of anti-Negro preju-

[15] The one significant exception to this statement is the pro-Negro activity on the part of the Catholic church, which came to St. Louis in the form of the Archbishop's ordering the abolition of segregation in the parochial schools and appeared in the similar change in the Jesuit-controlled St. Louis University. We have already seen that Catholic members tend to be somewhat more liberal than Protestant members regarding social relations with Negroes. It would seem that the influence of the church combined with the influence of the union in their case to make them somewhat more liberal.

TABLE 38. CHANGES IN THE ATTITUDES OF UNION MEMBERS TOWARD NEGROES AND JEWS

Answer	Percentage of Members Giving Indicated Answer			
	Toward Negroes		Toward Jews	
Questions: "Have your attitudes toward Negroes [Jews] changed since you became a member of the union? [If 'yes'] How so?"				
"Yes"	12.9		5.6	
"Much more friendly"		1.9		2.3
"Somewhat more friendly"		9.9		2.5
"Somewhat less friendly"		0.6		0.5
"Much less friendly"		0.5		0.3
"No"	85.5		91.8	
"Don't know"	1.1		0.8	
No answer	0.5		1.8	
Total	100.0		100.0	
Number	373 *		392	

* Negro members were not asked the question regarding Negroes.

dice in American society in general and in St. Louis in particular.

Another type of evidence we shall have to consider is the relation between ethnic attitude and length of membership in the union. We shall first take up the questions on change in attitude just presented. In attitudes toward Negroes, we find significant changes among the shop stewards – mostly in the friendly direction, but also in the less friendly direction (Table 39). In attitudes toward both Negroes and Jews, among rank-and-file members the group which has been in the union from one to three years express most change. Again we see that it is *not* the members who have been in the union longest who are most liberal, as we might have expected them to be if we considered union policy to be the only influence promoting change in ethnic attitudes.

Probing further into the relationship between length of membership in the union and ethnic attitudes, we may examine Table 40. On the question of having Negroes on the union staff, the members who have been in the union from one to three years are most in favor of it, but they are also among those most against it. On the question of having Jews

TABLE 39. CHANGES IN ATTITUDES TOWARD NEGROES AND JEWS IN RELATION TO LENGTH OF MEMBERSHIP IN THE UNION

	Percentage Expressing Indicated Change in Attitude					
			Of Nonstewards, Grouped by Years in Union			
Change in Attitude	Of All Members	Of Shop Stewards	Less than 1	1–3	4–10	Over 10
Toward Negroes						
"Much more friendly"	1.9	3.2	2.3	1.4	1.3	...
"Somewhat more friendly"	9.9	14.5	9.1	13.7	7.8	6.9
"Somewhat less friendly"	0.6	3.2	...	...	...	...
"Much less friendly"	0.5	1.6	...	...	0.6	...
Total saying "yes" to change	12.9	22.5	11.4	15.1	9.7	6.9
Computed on base of	373 *	62	44	73	159	29
Toward Jews						
"Much more friendly"	2.3	3.1	2.3	2.7	2.3	...
"Somewhat more friendly"	2.5	...	4.6	5.4	2.3	...
"Somewhat less friendly"	0.5	...	...	1.4	0.6	...
"Much less friendly"	0.3	...	...	...	0.6	...
Total saying "yes" to change	5.6	3.1	6.9	9.5	5.8	0.0
Computed on base of	392	64	44	74	172	31

* Negro members were not asked the questions regarding Negroes.

on the union staff, these members are not so strongly in favor of it and are most against it; thus the findings are not consistent with those from the previous table. The position of the oldest members is mostly that of not caring either way as to whether there are Negroes and Jews on the union staff. This could not be called an antiminority position. On the question about using Negroes on the picket line, it is the oldest members who are most equalitarian: 44.8 per cent of

TABLE 40. ATTITUDES TOWARD HAVING NEGROES AND JEWS ON THE UNION STAFF IN RELATION TO LENGTH OF MEMBERSHIP IN THE UNION

Answer	Distribution of Answers by Percentage				
	Of Nonstewards, Grouped by Years in Union				
	Less than 1	1–3	4–10	Over 10	Of Shop Stewards
Question: "What do you think of having Negroes on the union staff?"					
"Good idea"	20.4	27.4	27.0	17.2	53.2
"Bad idea"	43.2	39.7	34.6	27.6	19.4
"Don't care either way"	34.1	32.9	36.5	51.7	27.4
"Don't know"; no answer	2.3	...	1.9	3.5	...
Total	100.0	100.0	100.0	100.0	100.0
Number	44	73	159	29	62
Question: "What do you think of having Jews on the union staff?"					
"Good idea"	43.2	29.7	40.1	22.6	54.7
"Bad idea"	11.4	17.6	7.6	9.7	3.1
"Don't care either way"	45.4	51.4	51.2	64.5	42.2
"Don't know"; no answer	...	1.3	1.1	3.2	...
Total	100.0	100.0	100.0	100.0	100.0
Number	44	74	172	31	64
Question: "Do you think it is a good idea or a bad idea to have Negroes on a picket line along with whites?"					
"Good idea"	25.0	30.1	27.7	44.8	45.2
"Doesn't make any difference"	50.0	39.7	44.7	31.0	38.7
"Bad idea"	25.0	28.8	26.4	20.7	14.5
"Don't know"; no answer	...	1.4	1.2	3.5	1.6
Total	100.0	100.0	100.0	100.0	100.0
Number	44	73	159	29	62

them think it is a good idea to have Negroes on a picket line along with whites, as compared with only 25.0 per cent among the newest members. While fewer of the oldest members give the neutral response which can also be considered unprejudiced, fewer of them also give the prejudiced response that it is a "bad idea" to have Negroes on a picket line along with whites. It is to be observed that these questions are in the area of internal union relations, and, as we have noted, it is in this area that the union generally has its greatest effect on the attitudes of its most loyal members.

Turning to the matter of general stereotypes, the evidence is conflicting as to whether older members show themselves to be less anti-Semitic than newer members. Answers to two questions regarding the general treatment of Jews are associated with length of membership in the union in Table 41.

TABLE 41. ATTITUDES TOWARD THE TREATMENT OF JEWS IN BUSINESS IN RELATION TO LENGTH OF MEMBERSHIP IN THE UNION

	Distribution of Attitudes by Percentage				
	Of Nonstewards, Grouped by Years in Union				
Attitude Expressed	Less than 1	1–3	4–10	Over 10	Of Shop Stewards
Statement: "It would be a good idea if more business concerns would refuse to hire Jews."					
"Agree"	9.1	10.8	7.0	3.2	1.6
"Disagree"	72.7	63.5	68.0	54.9	81.2
"Can't decide"	18.2	23.0	23.3	41.9	17.2
No answer	...	2.7	1.7	...	...
Total	100.0	100.0	100.0	100.0	100.0
Number	44	74	172	31	64
Statement: "It would be a good idea if Jews were prevented from getting more power in the business world."					
"Agree"	25.0	35.1	26.2	16.1	28.1
"Disagree"	59.1	41.9	49.4	54.9	62.5
"Can't decide"	15.9	20.3	22.7	25.8	9.4
No answer	...	2.7	1.7	3.2	...
Total	100.0	100.0	100.0	100.0	100.0
Number	44	74	172	31	64

The proportion disagreeing with the proposition about job discrimination against Jews descends from 72.7 per cent among the newest members to 54.9 per cent among the oldest members. On the other hand, the proportion agreeing also decreased from 9.1 per cent to 3.2 per cent. On the proposition about curtailing the economic power of Jews, the trend from newest to oldest members is irregular, but in general it falls. But again the proportion agreeing with the discriminatory statement also falls. The older members tend more to be in doubt whether or not they should be anti-Semitic.

Thus no consistent conclusions can be drawn from these various data on the relationship between prejudice and length of membership in the union. This might suggest that answers to these questions are not highly reliable; on the other hand, the inconsistency may be only superficial, and a more complicated relationship would satisfactorily explain it. The following is tentatively offered as a solution which will be supported by a partial test. We have noted that those of the rank and file who say they have become friendly toward minorities since joining the union are most frequently to be found among members who have been in the union from one to three years. Since these are neither the newest nor the oldest members, it can be neither the union's influence nor the outside forces impinging on youth which alone explain the change in ethnic attitude. But it could be a combination of both these factors. That is, the union could be having an effect on all its members; but young people generally are more liberal than older people. If both these things are true, the greatest changes would naturally be evidenced among those who have been in the union a while but not so long that they are old. This could be the group that has been in the union from one to three years.

The oldest members tend to be most against economic and social equality for minorities. But the union's equalitarian policy has its greatest effect not in these fields, as we noted in the first four sections of this chapter, but rather in the field of internal union relations. The oldest members have the greatest solidarity with the union,[16] and therefore it may be expected that insofar as they have any ethnic liberalism, it will show up in answers to questions about the integration of minorities into the union. This we have seen to be the case in the questions both about the use of minority members on the staff and on the picket line. Our explanation of the apparent inconsistency in the relationship between ethnic liberalism and longevity thus runs as follows: The union's equalitarian policy is having some effect, but this effect is complicated by an outside factor which works in the same direction. The outside factor is the general change in the

[16] See Chapter VII, Section B, for evidence on this point.

climate of opinion in the United States with respect to minorities. The only way to separate these two influences is to note how they affect different groups within the union differently. The "general climate of opinion" factor affects the younger people the most, and it encourages them to be more liberal in general economic and social relations. The "union policy" factor has the greatest effect on those who have been in the union for some time, and it encourages them primarily to be equalitarian within the union.

TABLE 42. ETHNIC ATTITUDES OF UNION MEMBERS AND LONGEVITY IN THE UNION, WITH AGE HELD CONSTANT

	Distribution of Answers by Percentage, According to Age and Longevity					
	29 Years and Under		30 to 49 Years		50 Years and Older	
Answer	In Union Less than 4 Years	In Union 4 Years or Longer	In Union Less than 4 Years	In Union 4 Years or Longer	In Union Less than 4 Years *	In Union 4 Years or Longer
Question: "What do you think of having Jews on the union staff?"						
"Good idea" ..	34.6	31.4	42.9	42.2	23.1	46.1
"Bad idea"	9.0	5.9	17.1	6.9	38.5	6.7
"Don't care either way" ..	56.4	62.7	37.1	48.3	38.4	46.1
"Don't know"; no answer ...	...	...	2.9	2.6	...	1.1
Total	100.0	100.0	100.0	100.0	100.0	100.0
Number	78	51	35	116	13	89
Question: "Do you think it is a good idea or a bad idea for your union to try to get Negroes into jobs in the place where you work when there are vacancies?"						
"Good idea" ...	14.1	5.9	17.1	20.7	7.7	21.4
"Bad idea"	34.6	43.1	34.3	38.8	69.2	47.2
"O.K. up to a point"	50.0	43.1	42.9	29.3	23.1	23.6
"Don't know"; no answer ...	1.3	7.9	5.7	11.2	...	7.8
Total	100.0	100.0	100.0	100.0	100.0	100.0
Number	78	51	35	116	13	89

* The cases in this column are too few for reliable percentages, but the figures are presented nevertheless since they clearly fit into the general pattern.

This hypothesis fits the essential facts thus far presented about longevity and ethnic attitudes. It should be understood that neither factor is of dominant influence for the majority of members: neither force for ethnic liberalism is as powerful as the general culture pattern of ethnic prejudice. Thus their influences are relatively weak as well as intertwined with each other. We offer as a partial test of this hypothesis the figures on ethnic attitudes of the various longevity groups within each age group (Table 42). By holding age constant in this way, we can see that longevity *is* intrinsically somewhat related to ethnic liberalism (for all the age groups indicated except the youngest on the question of getting jobs for Negroes). Therefore we have another evidence that the union is having some effect in creating ethnic liberalism among some of its members.

G. Some Further Correlates of Prejudice

The question on whether or not the union should try to get Negroes jobs in shops where white members work was cross-tabulated with many of the other questions, to see what significant associations there are with economic prejudice against Negroes.

The first finding has significance for workers' education. Those who are already most friendly toward Negroes are the ones who would be interested in an educational course on minority groups: 28.1 per cent of those who would have the union help Negroes get jobs, as compared to only 3.1 per cent of those who would not, are willing to take such a course. In other words, a course on minority groups would serve largely to confirm liberal attitudes rather than to change the minds of the prejudiced.

As has been discovered in several other studies, liberalism toward Negroes is associated with liberalism on other issues. For example, those most willing to have the union help Negroes get jobs are also most willing to have women on the union staff.[17] Another example is shown by the figures in

[17] The figures on this point are presented in Section H of this chapter.

Table 43. Those most willing to have the union help Negroes are also the ones most likely to disagree with the proposition that Jews and Catholics should not hold high political office. Of course, these correlations are far from perfect even though they are significant.

TABLE 43. ATTITUDES OF UNION MEMBERS TOWARD NEGROES RELATED TO THEIR ATTITUDES TOWARD JEWS AND CATHOLICS

Attitude Expressed	Percentage Expressing Indicated Attitude, According to Attitude toward Negroes: For Union's Helping Negroes Get Jobs	For Union's Helping Negroes "Up to a point"	Against Union's Helping Negroes Get Jobs
Statement: "Jews should not be allowed to hold high political office."			
"Agree"	9.4	11.7	21.5
"Disagree"	82.8	59.9	55.2
"Can't decide"	7.8	26.3	22.7
"Don't know"; no answer	...	2.1	0.6
Total	100.0	100.0	100.0
Number	64	163	137
Statement: "Catholics should not be allowed to hold high political office."			
"Agree"	6.2	8.0	8.6
"Disagree"	84.4	70.1	71.8
"Can't decide"	9.4	20.4	18.4
"Don't know"; no answer	...	1.5	1.2
Total	100.0	100.0	100.0
Number	64	163	137

When white members are classified according to the type of job they have, it may be seen that clerical workers are more willing to have the union help Negroes get jobs, manufacturing workers (especially in candy manufacturing) are less willing, and no significant differences appear for the bulk of the union members, who are engaged in distribution work. Among those willing to have the union help Negroes, office workers constitute 26.6 per cent and manufacturing workers 14.1 per cent. Among those not willing to have the union help Negroes, office workers constitute only 15.3 per cent, but manufacturing workers make up 22.1 per cent.

We have already noted that white Catholics in the union are more willing to have social relations with Negroes than are white Protestants, although nonchurchgoers are most liberal of all in this respect. The same differentials hold for attitudes toward economic equality for Negroes, but there are practically no differences between religious groups with respect to anti-Semitism. These facts are shown in Table 44.

TABLE 44. RELIGIOUS DIFFERENTIALS AMONG WHITE UNION MEMBERS IN PREJUDICE AGAINST NEGROES AND JEWS

Response	Distribution of Responses by Percentage: Of Church-Attending Catholics	Of Church-Attending Protestants	Of Nonchurch-goers of Catholic or Protestant Background
Question: "Do you think it is a good idea or a bad idea for your union to try to get Negroes into all kinds of jobs in the place where you work, including good jobs, when there are vacancies and Negroes have seniority?"			
"Good idea"	23.7	13.5	31.0
"Bad idea"	51.1	49.6	39.4
"O.K. up to a point"	20.8	34.6	28.2
"Don't know"; no answer	4.4	2.3	1.4
Total	100.0	100.0	100.0
Number	135	133	71
Statement: "It would be a good idea to keep Jews out of Christian neighborhoods."			
"Agree"	8.1	9.8	8.4
"Disagree"	70.4	69.2	74.7
"Can't decide"	20.0	20.3	16.9
"Don't know"; no answer	1.5	0.7	...
Total	100.0	100.0	100.0
Number	135	133	71

On the question of the union's helping to get promotions for Negroes, 23.7 per cent of the Catholics are definitely affirmative, as compared to only 13.5 per cent of the Protestants but 31.0 per cent of the nonchurchgoers. There is no difference between Catholics and Protestants in the proportion against the union's helping Negroes get promotions, but on other questions Catholics are slightly more liberal toward Negroes also. On the question regarding the residential segregation of Jews, there are practically no differences between Catholics, Protestants, and nonchurchgoers; about 8–9 per cent of all groups definitely favor it and about 17–20 per cent more cannot decide.

We have already presented some evidence that there is only a very slight relationship between wanting democracy in the union and being liberal in favoring social relations with Negroes. Another evidence that desiring democracy in the union and ethnic liberalism are somewhat related is provided by Table 45. The figures there show that, while around 11 per cent of those who want the director or the stewards' council to run the union are anti-Semitic, only about 6 per cent of those who want the rank and file to run the union are anti-Semitic.

The greater ethnic liberalism of the more educated members has already been mentioned with respect to Negroes. There is also a definite relationship between better education and liberalism in attitudes toward Jews. The figures showing the proportions, among members of differing educational backgrounds, that favor residential segregation of Negroes and Jews are given in Table 46. In all educational-status groups the proportion favoring the residential segregation of Negroes is overwhelmingly higher than the proportion favoring the residential segregation of Jews. But about 9–10 per cent more of the most poorly educated group than of the best educated group favor segregation for both Negroes and Jews. As the table shows, 11.2 per cent of those with only a grade-school education definitely favor residential segregation of Jews, and 19.8 per cent more cannot decide. These figures are to be compared with the 1.2 per cent of the high-school graduates or "some college" group who definitely favor residential segregation of Jews and the 9.8 per cent who cannot decide.

H. Attitudes toward Women in the Union

Women are not an ethnic group, of course. But in a union or work situation they may be discriminated against, and in

TABLE 45. RELATIONSHIP BETWEEN THE DESIRE FOR DEMOCRACY IN THE UNION AND LIBERALISM TOWARD JEWS

Attitude toward Jews	Percentage Expressing Indicated Attitude toward Jews, According to Attitude toward Democracy in the Union — "Would you rather have important matters affecting the union be decided by the		
	Union Director	Stewards' Council	Rank-and-File Members
Statement: "It would be a good idea to keep Jews out of Christian neighborhoods."			
"Agree"	11.1	10.6	5.9
"Disagree"	74.1	70.3	73.2
"Can't decide"	14.8	17.0	20.5
No answer	...	2.1	0.4
Total	100.0	100.0	100.0
Number	27	94	254

TABLE 46. RELATIONSHIP BETWEEN THE EDUCATIONAL BACKGROUNDS OF UNION MEMBERS AND THEIR ATTITUDES ON THE RESIDENTIAL SEGREGATION OF NEGROES AND JEWS

Attitude on Residential Segregation	Percentage Expressing Indicated Attitude, According to Educational Level		
	Grade-School Education	Some High School but Not Graduated	High School Graduate or College
Question: "Do you think that Negroes should be permitted to live in the same block with white persons?"			
"Yes"	12.1	11.7	21.3
"No"	85.2	86.5	76.2
"Don't know"; no answer	2.7	1.8	2.5
Total	100.0	100.0	100.0
Number	182	111	80
Statement: "It would be a good idea to keep Jews out of Christian neighborhoods."			
"Agree"	11.2	8.8	1.2
"Disagree"	68.0	64.6	89.0
"Can't decide"	19.8	24.8	9.8
No answer	1.0	1.8	...
Total	100.0	100.0	100.0
Number	198	113	82

this sense are a minority group. In this section we shall see what the members' attitudes are toward having women as shop stewards or staff members.[18] The over-all percentages and the percentages for various age and sex groups are shown in Table 47. Women members are only somewhat more in favor of a woman as shop steward or on the staff than are men members. In general, a majority (57.1 per cent) of the members think there should be women on the

TABLE 47. ATTITUDES OF UNION MEMBERS TOWARD WOMEN AS SHOP STEWARDS OR STAFF MEMBERS, ACCORDING TO SEX AND AGE

	Distribution of Answers by Percentage						
	Of All Members	Of Men, by Age			Of Women, by Age		
Answer		Under 30	30–49	50 and Over	Under 30	30–49	50 and Over *
Question: "In general, is it better to have a woman or man as a shop steward?"							
"Woman"	1.8	...	...	1.2	2.0	3.8	8.7
"Man"	29.6	35.1	31.7	35.0	29.4	17.0	26.1
"Makes no difference if person is capable"	43.6	45.4	37.6	40.0	54.9	50.9	34.8
"Depends on whether workers are men or women"	24.0	16.9	30.7	23.8	13.7	26.4	30.4
No answer	1.0	2.6	...	...	...	1.9	...
Total	100.0	100.0	100.0	100.0	100.0	100.0	100.0
Number	392	77	101	80	51	53	23
Question: "What do you think of having women on the union staff?"							
"Good idea"	57.1	36.4	51.5	70.0	72.5	67.9	52.2
"Bad idea"	12.7	11.7	22.8	6.3	5.9	5.7	21.7
"Don't care either way"	28.8	51.9	24.7	21.2	21.6	18.9	26.1
"Don't know"; no answer	1.4	...	1.0	2.5	...	7.5	...
Total	100.0	100.0	100.0	100.0	100.0	100.0	100.0
Number	392	77	101	80	51	53	23

* The cases in the sample in this category are too few (only 23) for reliable percentages, but the figures are reported here because they fit into the pattern.

[18] At the time of the survey there was a woman on the union staff and there were a number of women serving as shop stewards.

union staff. But only a very small proportion (1.8 per cent) think it is preferable to have a woman as shop steward. The largest proportion (43.6 per cent) feel that it makes no difference whether the steward is a man or a woman provided the person is capable. Women members are somewhat more inclined to express this point of view than are men. Almost a fourth of the members (24.0 per cent) think the sex of a shop steward should be determined by the sex of the rank-and-file workers in the shop, and men are slightly more inclined to say this than are women.

Age differences on this issue are fairly marked. In general, the older the man the more partial he is toward having a woman on the staff, although it is the middle-aged men who are also most against the idea. Among women members, on the other hand, the younger ones are most in favor of having a woman on the staff. On the question about having women as shop stewards, older women are more positively in favor of it than younger women, and are also more inclined to want the sex of the shop membership to be the determining factor. Age differences among men are roughly the same as among women on answers to this question.

Answers to these questions in terms of the irrelevance of sex—that is, "makes no difference if person is capable" and "don't care either way"—might be considered to be the most democratic. As was pointed out, women are somewhat more inclined than men to give this answer with respect to having women as shop stewards, but men are more inclined to give this answer with respect to having women on the staff. In all cases the younger members were more inclined to give this answer than were the older members.

Another expression of attitudes toward women on the part of male union members is afforded by answers to the question, "Should wives and husbands of union members be invited to attend regular meetings?" Table 48 shows that twice as many members favor inviting spouses as are opposed to it—48.2 per cent compared to 24.2 per cent, with 26.3 per cent saying that they don't care either way. There is very little

TABLE 48. ATTITUDES OF UNION MEMBERS TOWARD INVITING SPOUSES TO ATTEND UNION MEETINGS

Answer	Of All Members	Of Men, by Age: Under 30	Of Men, by Age: 30–49	Of Men, by Age: 50 and Over	Of Women, by Age: Under 30	Of Women, by Age: 30–49	Of Women, by Age: 50 and Over *	Of Shop Stewards, Both Sexes
	Distribution of Answers by Percentage							
Question: "Should wives and husbands of union members be invited to attend regular meetings?"								
"Yes"	48.2	42.8	52.5	51.3	39.2	54.7	47.9	57.8
"No"	24.2	20.8	27.7	30.0	23.5	15.1	21.7	23.4
"Don't care either way" .	26.3	29.9	19.8	18.7	37.3	28.3	30.4	18.8
"Don't know"; no answer ..	1.3	6.5	...	...	...	1.9	...	...
Total	100.0	100.0	100.0	100.0	100.0	100.0	100.0	100.0
Number	392	77	101	80	51	53	23	64

* This column is based on too few cases for reliable percentages.

difference between men and women members in their answers to this question; if anything, men members are more favorable to the idea of inviting spouses to union meetings than are women members. This is additional evidence that there is no difference between men and women members in prejudice against women. Age differences are inconsistent and cannot be generalized about. Shop stewards are more in favor of inviting spouses to union meetings than are rank-and-file members.

The question can be raised whether prejudice against women is related to prejudice against a racial minority like Negroes. This relationship does exist among the union members, demonstrating that a negative attitude toward women in the union is really prejudice. The relationship may come as a surprise to some, perhaps especially to those who are prejudiced, but it is well known to social scientists. The figures are shown in Table 49. Of those who think it is a bad idea for the union to help Negroes get jobs, 18.9 per cent also think it is a bad idea to have women on the union staff, as compared to only 4.7 per cent among those who think it is

TABLE 49. RELATIONSHIP BETWEEN THE ATTITUDES OF UNION MEMBERS TOWARD NEGROES AND THEIR ATTITUDES TOWARD WOMEN

	Percentage Expressing Indicated Attitude toward Women, According to Attitude toward Negroes		
	Question: "Do you think it is a good idea or a bad idea for your union to try to get Negroes into jobs in the place where you work when there are vacancies?"		
Attitude toward Women	"Good idea"	"Bad idea"	"O.K. up to a point"
Question: "What do you think of having women on the union staff?"			
"Good idea"	75.0	52.5	53.3
"Bad idea"	4.7	18.9	10.9
"Don't care either way"	20.3	28.0	32.9
"Don't know"; no answer	...	0.6	2.9
Total	100.0	100.0	100.0
Number	64	163	137
Question: "In general is it better to have a woman or a man as a shop steward?"			
"Woman"	1.6	1.8	2.2
"Man"	21.9	38.0	22.6
"Makes no difference if person is capable"	57.8	34.4	46.0
"Depends on whether workers are men or women"	18.7	23.9	29.2
"Don't know"; no answer	...	1.9	...
Total	100.0	100.0	100.0
Number	64	163	137

a good idea for the union to help Negroes. And among those who think it is a bad idea for the union to help Negroes get jobs, 38.0 per cent specify that it is better to have a man as shop steward, as compared to only 21.9 per cent among those who think it is a good idea for the union to help Negroes. Thus the association between attitudes toward women and attitudes toward Negroes is shown.

I. Summary

1. Attitudes toward Negroes among white union members in a purely social situation are largely negative, in a job situa-

tion are about evenly divided pro and con, and in a union situation are largely favorable. For example, 83.7 per cent do not think that Negroes should be allowed to live in the same block as whites; 44.2 per cent think it is a bad idea for the union to try to get jobs for Negroes where there are vacancies; but only 33.8 per cent think it is a bad idea to have Negroes on the union staff.

2. Unwillingness to have the union help get jobs for Negroes is almost solely a matter of personal antipathy to working with Negroes and is not due to a belief that this is not particularly a union function or a belief that it might be bad for Negroes.

3. The majority of union members are in favor of separate union social affairs for Negroes, but not by such a large proportion as they are in favor of social segregation outside the union situation.

4. Over half the members approve the union's policy with respect to minority groups, and over a third more don't know about it. Only 5.3 per cent say that the union spends too much time on Negroes, and these are mostly the older members.

5. Few members feel any antipathy toward working side by side with Jews, and few object to having Jews on the union staff. Only a like small proportion (6–10 per cent) subscribe completely to employment discrimination against Jews and residential segregation of them. However, larger proportions (an additional 20 per cent approximately) cannot decide on these questions and might be called potential anti-Semites.

6. When it comes to stereotypes about Jews' having too much power in business and politics, only a simple majority can be found to disagree. On the proposition that Jews should be prevented from getting more power in the business world, 26.8 per cent agree and another 20.1 per cent can't decide.

7. While the proportion of all members saying that Catholics should not be allowed to hold high political office is 7.6

per cent, when white Protestant churchgoers alone are examined the proportion is 12.0 per cent plus 24.8 per cent unable to decide. The proportion is about the same against Jews' holding high political office (14.8 per cent, with 22.2 per cent unable to decide).

8. About 12 per cent of the members say they have become friendlier to Negroes since joining the union, and 5 per cent say they have become friendlier to Jews. Other evidence that union policy has influenced some members in a pro-equalitarian direction includes: (*a*) the fact that more members are equalitarian in the union situation than in outside social relationships; (*b*) the fact that older members are more equalitarian in the union situation and younger members in outside situations; (*c*) the fact that within any age category those with more union seniority are more equalitarian; (*d*) the fact that there is little criticism of the union's prominority policy.

9. Liberalism in attitudes toward Negroes is associated with liberalism in attitudes toward Jews, Catholics, and women.

10. The following associations were found with attitudes toward Negroes: (*a*) By religion, Catholics are more liberal than Protestants, although nonchurchgoers are most liberal of all. (*b*) By type of job, clerical workers are more liberal, and manufacturing workers less liberal, than the average member. (*c*) By education, the more educated are the more liberal. (*d*) By attitude toward democracy in the union, those desiring rank-and-file control of the union are the more liberal. (*e*) By longevity, there is no consistent difference between newer and older members; if anything, the older members are less liberal. But when chronological age is held constant, length of membership *is* found to be associated with ethnic liberalism.

11. Almost 30 per cent of the members specify that it is better to have a man as shop steward, and 12.7 per cent say it is a bad idea to have a woman on the union staff. On the other hand, a majority (57.1 per cent) think it is a good idea

to have a woman on the union staff, and 43.6 per cent say that sex should be no criterion for a shop steward provided the person is capable. Women members are only somewhat more liberal than men members on these issues. Older men are more favorable than are younger men toward having a woman on the staff, but among women members the opposite is true. On the question regarding women as shop stewards, older people are more positively in favor of it. On the other hand, younger members are more inclined to feel that sex is irrelevant in picking either a shop steward or a staff member.

12. Almost half the members are positively in favor of inviting spouses to union meetings, and only one fourth against it. Shop stewards are more strongly in favor of it, but there is little consistent difference by age or sex among the members.

CHAPTER VI

The Role of the Union

This short chapter takes up certain miscellaneous attitudes of the members which further reveal their conception of the role of the union and their relation to it.

A. *Conceptions of the Union's Services and Methods*

Various union members have different ideas of what the main functions of the union should be. Insofar as the members are aware of their own conceptions of the union, answers to the question on the union's main function (as reported in Table 50) are one of the best expressions of these conceptions. There can be little doubt that most of the members see the main function of the union to be the traditional activity of collective bargaining to gain higher wages and better working conditions. However, there are significant minorities among the members who emphasize the recent supplementary functions of unions — to get security and health benefits, to engage in political action, and to organize the unorganized and create a solid union front. Answers to this question were analyzed for the various longevity groups, and the only consistent difference that appeared is that the older members give greater weight to gaining benefits outside the shop — free medical service, pensions, legal advice, and so on — as a function of the union.

The attitudes toward these "extra" services were explored with another question which raised a hurdle against them:

TABLE 50. ATTITUDES OF UNION MEMBERS REGARDING THE UNION'S MAIN FUNCTIONS

Answer	Percentage of Members *
Question: "What do you think are the main things your union should work for right now, either through collective bargaining or through social action in the community?"	
Higher wages and/or collective bargaining	33.7
Better working conditions in the shop	18.4
Benefits outside the shop, such as LHI †	9.4
Job security and seniority	8.4
Political action	5.4
Organizing the unorganized	5.1
Better employer-employee relationships	3.8
General and community welfare	3.1
Miscellaneous	6.1
Nothing	4.9
"Don't know"	19.1
No answer	7.7
Number	392

* The percentages total more than 100 because some people gave more than one answer.

† LHI is the Labor Health Institute, the free medical service organization which the union secured for most of its members through collective bargaining with the employers.

TABLE 51. RELATIVE SUPPORT AMONG UNION MEMBERS FOR "EXTRA" UNION SERVICES

Answer	Percentage of Members
Question: "Do you think the union should put more time and money into getting higher wages from the employers or should it put more into a health plan, social and recreational activities, an insurance plan, and other things of that kind?"	
"More into higher wages"	24.3
"More into other things"	38.1
"About same amount"	35.7
"Don't know"; no answer	1.9
Total	100.0
Number	392

whether to prefer them or higher wages. The question and answers are reported in Table 51. The figures indicate that there is more support for the union's concentrating its efforts on getting these extra services than on getting wage raises.

The relative position of these two union functions is the opposite in Table 51 from what it is in Table 50, and we are faced with an inconsistency in the members' answers.

The simplest explanation of this inconsistency seems to be that the spontaneous answers of Table 50 are based partly on the traditional functions of unions – getting higher wages, shorter hours, and better conditions in the shop – answers that might naturally come to mind first when one is asked about the main purposes of a union. When asked to weigh these traditional functions against the "supplementary" ones – getting security for the worker and his family, providing opportunity for social and recreational activities – the workers give greater weight to the latter. This suggests that the members of this union feel a greater need for the latter functions but have not been fully educated to think in terms other than the traditional ones.[1] Partial support for this interpretation comes out of the fact that the more educated members of the union are somewhat more in favor of the supplementary functions than are the poorly educated members, even though the better educated members probably are less in need of security and social-recreational opportunities.

A question about how often the union should use the strike reveals something of what the members think the union's methods should be, as distinguished from its goals. A substantial majority (63.5 per cent) of the members are willing to use the strike as often as needed to secure the goals of the union. Only a very small proportion (4.1 per cent) think of the strike primarily as a means of demonstrating power and would have it used frequently whether it is needed at the time or not. At the other extreme, only 16.8 per cent would have the union practically never employ a strike.[2] There are no significant, consistent differences in the answers to this question among members who have been in the union for

[1] Another factor to be considered is that many workers feel that their wages are as high as they can get now, but that they *can* get the supplementary benefits by union activity now.

[2] The remaining members include 13.5 per cent who would use the strike once in a while, and 2.1 per cent who say "Don't know" or give no answer.

varying lengths of time or between shop stewards and rank-and-file members.

B. Attitudes toward the Union Contract and the Processing of Grievances

The union contract is the central means through which many of the union's goals are realized and to gain which the strike and other union techniques are employed. About three fifths of the members think the union has secured a good contract for them (Table 52). Only 1.5 per cent think the contract is a bad one.[3] There is a significant relationship between knowledge of the contract and approval of it. Whereas only 45.6 per cent of those who did not read the contract think it is a good one, 72.5 per cent of those who read and

TABLE 52. ATTITUDES OF UNION MEMBERS TOWARD THE CONTRACT AS RELATED TO THEIR KNOWLEDGE ABOUT IT

	Distribution of Answers by Percentage, According to Knowledge of Contract				
Answer	Of All Members	Of Those Who Did Not Read Contract	Of Those Who Read Contract but Understood Only Part of It	Of Those Who Read Contract and Understood Most of It	Of Those Who Read Contract and Understood All of It
Question: "From what you know of the contract, is it a good one, a bad one, or just average?"					
"Good"	59.2	45.6	53.1	71.1	72.5
"Bad"	1.5	0.8	1.6	1.6	2.9
"Average"	29.6	29.6	43.8	27.3	23.2
"Don't know"; no answer	9.7	24.0	1.5	...	1.4
Total	100.0	100.0	100.0	100.0	100.0
Number	392 *	125	64	128	69

* The total number includes six persons who did not respond to the question about reading the contract.

[3] Since the members are in fifteen different shops, they have fifteen different contracts, and some contracts are likely to be better or worse than others.

understood all of it think it is a good one. Of course, many of those who did not read the contract did not approve of it because they did not know enough about it (24.0 per cent said, "Don't know," or gave no answer). But a more serious problem exists for those who read the contract but understood "little or none of it" or "some of it." Only 53.1 per cent of these members thought the contract was a good one. Here is clear indication that the union would gain in strength and solidarity if the contract were made clear and understandable to all members.

Next to collective bargaining and the formulation of the contract, the most important traditional function of the union has always been to get justice for a member when he has a grievance against the employer. Most grievances are based upon some real or alleged violation of the contract by the employer. Thus handling grievances is the day-to-day putting into effect of the contract. When a worker thinks he has a grievance, he tells his shop steward about it and the steward takes it up with the foreman. If the shop steward and the foreman fail to agree, they appeal to progressively higher authorities: The shop steward may go to the chief shop steward (who is the union leader for the whole plant), to a staff member at the central union office, or even to the union's director. The foreman may go to the plant superintendent, or to one of the company's top officials. In rare cases when there is no agreement at the top level, the company and the union may agree to let the case be decided by an impartial outside arbitrator. There may be a strike over a grievance, but practically always the strike is reserved as a weapon for use in contract negotiations rather than in grievance settlement.

While this "grievance machinery" may be complex, depending on the size and structure of the union and the company and on the provisions of the contract, most grievances are handled simply by the shop steward and the foreman, and therefore a large amount of the satisfaction and security which the ordinary member gets out of the union depends

TABLE 53. OPINIONS OF RANK-AND-FILE UNION MEMBERS ABOUT THE ABILITY OF THE SHOP STEWARD

Answer	Distribution of Answers by Percentage				
	Of All Rank-and-File Members	Of Rank-and-File Members Grouped by Years in Union			
		Less than 1	1–3	4–10	Over 10
Question: "Does your steward do a good job, fair job, or poor job of handling grievances?"					
"Good job"	68.9	59.1	64.9	72.7	74.2
"Fair job"	21.9	27.3	23.0	20.3	19.3
"Poor job"	5.5	6.8	8.1	4.1	6.5
"Don't know"; no answer	3.7	6.8	4.0	2.9	...
Total	100.0	100.0	100.0	100.0	100.0
Number	328	44	74	172	31

on the ability of his shop steward. A question was asked in the survey about how good the member thought his steward was in handling grievances (Table 53). Two thirds of the rank-and-file members were well pleased with the steward's performance, and almost 22 per cent more thought he did a fair job. Only 5.5 per cent thought he did a poor job. Older members were somewhat more satisfied than newer members.

Certain questions asked in the questionnaire were designed to bring out criticisms of union activities and suggestions for improvement. They do not cover all union activities but only a few selected ones. Only a small proportion of those interviewed answered these questions, so that the answers cannot be presumed to represent typical or majority opinion. They are simply suggestions made by a few of the members.

One of the questions of the type designed to evoke spontaneous comments was, "Do you have any suggestions for improving the handling of grievances?" Several of the members answered that grievances should be handled more quickly. One said, for example, "Take them up as soon as they happen. Don't cool off." Another answered, "The matter should be settled right away, not delayed." A second type of comment that came up several times concerned the quality of the grievance handling. Most of the criticisms were directed at the ability of the shop stewards. One member said that "the stewards should talk up to the bosses," and in another shop a member referred to the steward with the remark, "We need someone with enough nerve." In two other shops members made more specific suggestions: "The shop steward should be permitted to talk directly to the company president." "Our steward hesitates to call on the union staff and thus loses to the boss."

Other criticisms of stewards included several charges of ignorance and one of closeness to the management. Yet in another shop the staff was blamed: "Staff members should take a more active part." Members from two different shops thought there should be more frequent grievance meetings or labor-management round tables. Still other members complained about the sex and race representation on grievance committees, or about the lack of representation of the member with the grievance. Several members expressed the opinion that too many people take part in the discussion of the grievance, that it could be handled better if the member with a grievance got in touch with the steward alone.

C. Criticisms of the Union Staff

In Chapter III we considered, in connection with the discussion of union loyalty, several of the members' criticisms of the union staff. To complete the picture, we shall here consider two other bases of criticism. In private conversation it has been said that some staff members lead immoral lives. To determine whether or not this was a common feeling among the rank and file, the following question was asked: "Do you think the union staff members' conduct is what it should be? (Do they behave properly?)" Only 5.2 per cent had any complaint to make (although 16.3 per cent more said, "Don't know," and another 3.8 per cent gave no answer). The single most important criticism here voiced—by only 1.8 per cent of the total membership, however—is that the staff members are given to swearing. A few other members criticized the staff for drinking, gambling, and "loose living." Two members said that some of the staff were domineering, and one each criticized the staff for "cutting up at union meetings," for being "too tough," and for not being religious enough. On the whole, then, this type of criticism does not loom as important in the members' minds.

Another question turns up a larger number of critics, although we have no way of telling how serious the matter is for the members who criticize. This has to do with the hiring of some of the staff from outside the union and outside the city. At the time of the survey at least six of the staff members, including the union's director, had been St. Louisans for only a few years. Several of these had been sent in originally by the former International union — the United Retail, Wholesale, and Department Store Employees union — which some members had always disliked and been suspicious of. As recently as the time of the survey, more than a third (37.0 per cent) of the members did not like the idea of bringing in staff from outside the union and outside the city.[4]

There may not seem to be much difference between those who say the union is very well run and those who say it is fairly well run, but this difference is reflected in some variation in the enthusiasm for the noneconomic functions of the union (Table 54). Those who find the union to be very well run include larger proportions of those willing to have the union participate more in new organization and in politics. The difference for each question is about 10–12 per cent of the respective groups. It is impossible to tell which way the causation runs, but it seems clear that there is some association between an enthusiasm for the union management and a willingness to have the union grow and engage in political action.

[4] Of the rest, 19.6 per cent said it is a good idea to have staff members who come from outside St. Louis; 40.8 per cent "don't care either way"; 2.6 per cent "don't know" or give no answer.

TABLE 54. ATTITUDES OF UNION MEMBERS TOWARD THE NONECONOMIC FUNCTIONS OF THE UNION, AS RELATED TO THEIR EVALUATION OF UNION MANAGEMENT

Attitude toward Noneconomic Functions	Evaluation of How Union is Run: Percentage Saying "Very well"	Evaluation of How Union is Run: Percentage Saying "Fairly well"
Question: "How much time and money should your union put into organizing workers in places where there is no union now?"		
"A great deal"	44.4	32.4
"Some"	44.9	54.9
"Very little"	0.5	2.3
"None at all"	2.7	2.3
"Don't know"; no answer	7.5	8.1
Total	100.0	100.0
Number	187	173
Question: "How much time and money should your union put into getting candidates elected to public office who are friendly to labor?"		
"A great deal"	35.8	24.9
"Some"	48.1	54.3
"Very little"	3.2	9.8
"None at all"	7.0	5.2
"Don't know"; no answer	5.9	5.8
Total	100.0	100.0
Number	187	173
Question: "Should the union help to start a Labor party some time in the future?"		
"Yes"	50.3	40.5
"No"	39.0	49.7
"Don't know"; no answer	10.7	9.8
Total	100.0	100.0
Number	187	173

Differential attitudes toward union management are related not only to attitudes toward the expansionist noneconomic functions of the union but also to specific criticisms of the union, as would be expected. This is illustrated by the fact that 65.2 per cent of those with the greatest enthusiasm for union management think all staff members are doing a good job, but only 45.7 per cent of those somewhat less enthusiastic have this opinion regarding staff members.[5]

[5] These figures are from answers to the question as to how well the members think their union is run. Those who think the union is run not so well or is run poorly are too few in number to tabulate.

D. Ambitions of the Members

The great majority of the members see the union as an instrument for achieving common goals. Only a few think of it as an avenue to leadership or personal promotion. This is shown in answers to a question asking whether the member ever thought of trying to become a union officer or staff member (Table 55). Those who think, occasionally or often,

TABLE 55. AMBITION TO BECOME A UNION LEADER, AS RELATED TO BELIEF ABOUT CHANCES FOR ADVANCEMENT

Answer to Question: "Have you ever thought of trying to become a union officer or staff member?"	Distribution of Answers by Percentage			
		Of Members with Specified Belief as to Their Chances of Becoming Foreman or Shop Owner		
	Of All Members	"No chance at all"	"Very small chance"	"Fair or good chance"
"Yes, often"	5.3	4.2	5.1	7.4
"Yes, occasionally"	10.4	3.1	11.2	16.1
"No, never"	83.3	92.2	82.7	76.5
"Don't know"; no answer	1.0	0.5	1.0	...
Total	100.0	100.0	100.0	100.0
Number	392 *	192	98	81

* The total number includes twenty-one persons who did not answer the question about the expected chances for advancement.

of trying to become a union official are also the ones who are more likely to think they have a fair or good chance of rising in the management scale. Whereas only 7.3 per cent of those who think they have no chance at all to become a foreman or shop owner have any desire to become a union official, 23.5 per cent of those who believe they have a good or fair chance at job promotion have this desire. It would thus seem that a general belief in one's own capacity exists, and those who want to become union leaders have this belief. It does *not* appear to be true that those who are most disgruntled because they believe the avenue toward promotion in the management scale is closed are the ones who want to become union leaders. Turning the figures another way, we find that only 28.5 per cent of those who have aspirations toward union leadership believe they have no chance at all to become a foreman or shop owner, even though about half[6] of all the members have this latter belief.

E. The Organization of Meetings and Social Affairs

The members were asked how they preferred the union's meetings and social affairs to be organized. The answers are shown in Table 56. Only 2 per cent take advantage of the opportunity to say that they do not want any kind of union meeting — which reinforces our earlier findings that the great majority of the members feel the need of a union and want the union to be democratic. The majority preference is for

TABLE 56. PREFERENCES OF UNION MEMBERS REGARDING THE ORGANIZATION OF UNION MEETINGS AND SOCIAL AFFAIRS

Type of Organization	Percentage of Members Preferring the Indicated Type of Organization: For Union Meetings	For Social Affairs *
Crew meetings (not over 25 people)	20.9	4.8
Shop meetings (all people who work for the company)	54.3	25.3
Meetings of workers in several shops (all people in one industry)	5.4	7.7
City-wide union meetings (all members of Teamsters Local 688)	11.0	53.8
Members of the same age group regardless of where they work	...†	2.8
No kind of union meeting	2.0	...†
Don't know; no answer	6.4	5.6
Total	100.0	100.0
Number	392	392

* The checklist answers are taken from the question regarding meetings; equivalent answers with a slightly different wording were used for the question regarding social affairs.

† This answer was not included in the checklist for this specific question.

[6] Of all those who give an answer to the question, "What chance do you think you have for getting ahead and becoming a foreman or shop owner yourself some day?" 52 per cent say, "No chance at all." However, 5.1 per cent give no answer to this question, and 0.3 per cent say, "Don't know," so of the *total* sample it is 48.7 per cent who say, "No chance at all." Another 24.7 per cent say, "Very small chance," 17.4 per cent say, "Fair chance," and the remaining 3.8 per cent say, "Good chance."

union meetings of shop size and social affairs of all-union size. In considering the latter point, it should be recalled (from Chapter V) that most members favor segregation of Negroes at union social affairs, and that therefore this preference for all-union social affairs means that they forget that some shops in the union are all-Negro or predominantly Negro. Organization by crews (25 members or less), which for a long while was a unique feature of this union, is favored by only a minority of the members. The older members and shop stewards prefer crew meetings more than do the newer members. The untried plans of organization by age or by industry (including several shops) get very little support.

The failure of the members to support the crew type of meeting is interesting in view of the favorable attention given it by certain outside observers. We may cite, for example, the comment of a local union leader in Chicago, Sidney Lens: "The United Distribution Workers in St. Louis, formerly with the CIO retail and wholesale union [shortly afterwards Teamsters Local 688], have organized a system of group meetings which is more important for the future of American labor than all the pronouncements of the big brass put together. The union, with 5,500 or 6,000 members, holds monthly group meetings of 25 workers each, staff members of the UDW actually meet with hundreds of small groups of this sort, talk to them on the evils of Taft-Hartley, immediate shop problems and the like, and listen to the members' complaints. The UDW is unquestionably the most dynamic CIO union in St. Louis; it can usually mobilize more men and women for a picket line and for a political door-ringing campaign than any other group in the city. Education of the rank and file has paid dividends. If its present policies continue, it will weather the storms of the future far better than other groups. Such methods of involving the rank and file are essential if labor is to move beyond its present status."[7]

[7] *Left, Right and Center: Conflicting Forces in American Labor* (Hinsdale, Ill.: H. Regnery Co., 1949), p. 417.

F. Miscellaneous Suggestions for Improving the Union

A general question at the end of the questionnaire was intended to allow the union member to say anything that he did not get a chance to say in answering the 120 previous questions. The question asked, "Is there anything else you would like to say about your union?" The answers include some compliments to the union and some derogatory remarks, but mostly consist of a variety of suggestions for improving the union as the commenting member sees it. Some of the suggestions are about broad policy; others are about small details. None should be given much weight: since each comment is made by only one person, it cannot be assumed to reflect a general attitude toward the union. The suggestions are listed below without comment:

The union brought wages up from $.65 per hour to $1.23.

Staff members should get some veterans on the staff for on-the-job training.

The union ought to separate into groups as crafts.

Staff officers could do more in getting more members into the LHI and in keeping closer track of rank-and-file members.

The Health Institute and health insurance should be dropped.

Members would rather have the money than the LHI.

The union feels too strongly about, and criticizes too much, any member who takes a job as foreman. He is regarded as a traitor.

There should be two large meetings or so per year instead of so many.

The union is now disorganized and the workers are dissatisfied. The men feel inhibited at meetings because women and children are present. The worker is forced to do what the employer wants, in subtle ways, without a fair chance to discuss it.

The men should stop talking about pushing the women out of the shop when jobs become scarce.

The union should devise a better dues-receipt system: now receipts are easily lost.

The union should not attempt to bully the company and protect lousy workers.

There should be more emphasis on spreading the union over the entire nation.

The union should take better care of its members instead of organizing new shops.

Nonmembers in shops should be forced to join.

Effort might be made to investigate the officers of the old union [i.e., old Teamsters Local 688] before we new ones come in.

The union should be kept democratic, to conform to American ideals. Lately the union has been trying to regiment thinking according to European class ideas.

The meeting should be held at 7:30 or 8:00 p.m.

The union collects dues before initiation.

Union finances should be controlled by the government; auditors are needed to cut down graft.

There should be beer parties for the guys after meetings three times a year.

The meetings should be on a new basis.

The union needs to organize new members and encourage inactives.

The union lets the company push it around.

The union should have its own building, do the employing itself, and lower dues to $2.00 in order to have a $1.00 fine for absence from meetings.

A pension plan should be worked out.

A provision is needed to vote "nonunion" persons out of the union.

Seniority should be stressed more.

Gibbons is a fine man.

The meetings should be later in the evening.

There should be strict shop stewards to keep the members in line.

The unions should organize store and white collar workers.

The union should see that contracts are signed without delay.

The union should develop its educational program more.

The union should help older workers to keep steady employment.

G. Summary

1. While the majority of the members see the main function of the union as that of gaining higher wages and better working conditions, significant minorities emphasize the recent supplementary functions of unions – to get security and health benefits, to engage in political action, and to create a solid union front of all workers. When confronted with the alternative of whether the union should concentrate on "higher wages" or on "other things," more members chose the latter.

2. The dominant attitude of the members toward the strike as a union technique is that it should be used as often as needed to get what the members want. Only 16.8 per cent say that it should practically never be used, and only 4.1 per cent would use it often, to prove power.

3. Almost 60 per cent of the members believe their contract is a good one, and only 1.5 per cent think it is a bad one (the others say it is "just average" or they do not know). Those who had read the contract and understood it were more likely to be favorable to it than those who had not.

4. Over two thirds of the members think their stewards do a good job of handling grievances, and only 5.5 per cent think they do a poor job.

5. Only 5.2 per cent have any complaint to make about the personal conduct of staff members, and their complaints vary. However, more than a third of the members think it is a bad idea for the union to bring in staff members from outside St. Louis.

6. Satisfaction with the union's management is related to the members' willingness to have the union engage in political activity and new organization.

7. The great majority of the members see the union as an instrument for achieving common goals. Only a few think of it as an avenue to leadership or personal promotion. Those who want to become union leaders are also likely to be the ones who think they have a chance to rise in the occupational scale to the position of foreman or shop owner.

8. The majority preference is for shop-wide union meetings and union-wide social affairs. Meetings or social affairs based on smaller units do not get much support, nor do untried plans (based on industry or age).

CHAPTER VII

The Attitudes of Special Groups of Members

A. Expected Differences between New and Old Members

One of the characteristics of a successful union is that it must educate its new members to follow the policies of the union. In most cases this implies that the long-time members of the union (those who have "longevity") will see things somewhat differently than do the new members. It was because of this premise that we examined the relationship between longevity and attitudes toward union issues in earlier chapters. By the accidents of nature and history, however, the relationship cannot be expected to be perfect. In the first place, there is naturally a relationship between longevity in the union and chronological age. Our whole society is undergoing such rapid change that there are generally major differences in attitudes between the old and the young. Thus the attitude of a new member of the union may be a function of his youth rather than of his newness in the union. Table 57 shows us the degree of relationship between age and longevity for the members of this union. A relationship definitely exists, although it is far from perfect. What is important is that the new members include few elderly people and that the old members include few young ones. The complication introduced by the relationship between age and longevity has already been seen in the examination of ethnic attitudes made in Chapter V, Section G.

TABLE 57. RELATIONSHIP BETWEEN LONGEVITY IN THE UNION AND CHRONOLOGICAL AGE

	Percentage of Members, Grouped by Years in Union				
Age, in Years	Under 1	1–3	4–6	7–10	Over 10
Under 20	26.0	13.9	3.0	...	...
20–29	50.0	41.8	22.8	21.9	2.1
30–39	10.9	24.1	11.9	25.7	14.6
40–49	2.2	11.4	27.7	22.8	33.4
50–59	8.7	6.3	14.8	13.4	20.8
60–69	2.2	2.5	14.8	12.4	20.8
70 and over	...	...	5.0	3.8	8.3
Total	100.0	100.0	100.0	100.0	100.0
Number *	46	79	101	105	48

* Six cases are excluded for lack of information on age, and seven cases are excluded for lack of information on longevity.

A second factor complicating any expected shift in attitude with increasing length of membership is the fact that workers become members in two distinctly different ways. When the union was organized in each shop, the majority of workers had to make up their minds voluntarily that they wanted a union. Since then new workers in each shop have joined the union, usually involuntarily after they got the job. Since all the shops in our study have been in the union for at least seven years, the older members are likely to be workers who formed a union voluntarily in times of unemployment, whereas the newer members are likely to be workers who joined the union involuntarily in times of labor shortage.[1] These factors must be borne in mind when considering the relationship between longevity and any particular attitude.

Shop stewards generally have been in the union for a number of years (at least in the shops we are considering, which have been organized for at least seven years).[2] But the stewards are different from other members who have

[1] When asked, "Why did you join the union?" 63.6 per cent of the members in the union less than one year spontaneously said they had to, whereas only 32.3 per cent of the members in the union over ten years gave this answer.

[2] Of the shop stewards and ex-shop stewards in the sample, 27 per cent had been in the union over 10 years, almost 40 per cent between 7 and 10 years, another 25 per cent between 4 and 6 years, and only 8 per cent 3 years or less.

been in the union for a long while, not only because of presumed capacities for leadership, but also because of the large number of union experiences they have had. They can be expected to be more loyal to the union and more aware of its problems and needs. For this reason shop stewards frequently have attitudes sharply different from those of other old members of the union and therefore will be singled out in the analysis of longevity in this chapter.

There have been occasions in the earlier chapters when it has been necessary to note the relationship between longevity and the subject then under discussion. These relationships will not be restated in this chapter; only new ones will be brought out.

B. How Older Members and Shop Stewards View Their Union and Its Problems

Older members and shop stewards are somewhat more loyal to the union, generally, than newer members are, but the critical minority among them is just as large. This is illustrated in Tables 58 and 60. In any general evaluation of how the union is run, shop stewards and older members have at least as large a proportion of critics as the newer group (11.0 per cent and 9.7 per cent respectively, as compared to 6.8 per cent among those in the union less than one year). On such a specific point as the number of meetings, the older members have the largest proportion (9.7 per cent) saying there are too many union meetings and the shop stewards the largest proportion (28.1 per cent) saying there are too few. Older members are about as likely as the rest to give negative answers to the question about whether the paid staff members are doing a good job. They are, however, more likely than the younger groups to say that *all* staff members (not just *most* of them) are doing a good job.

The desire for fewer meetings does not necessarily mean that older members have less interest in what the union is doing. On the contrary, they seem to have more interest. We have already seen in Table 20 that older members are more

TABLE 58. RELATIONSHIP BETWEEN LONGEVITY IN THE UNION AND CRITICISM OF THE UNION

Answer	Distribution of Answers by Percentage: Of Nonstewards, Grouped by Years in Union: Under 1	1–3	4–10	Over 10	Of Shop Stewards
Question: "In general, what do you think of the way your union is run?"					
"Very well"	43.2	39.2	48.8	45.2	53.1
"Fairly well"	43.2	51.3	45.3	45.1	35.9
"Not so well"	2.3	4.1	3.5	3.2	4.7
"Very poorly"	4.5	5.4	1.8	6.5	6.3
"Don't know"; no answer	6.8	...	0.6	...	...
Total	100.0	100.0	100.0	100.0	100.0
Number	44	74	172	31	64
Question: "Do you think there are too many union meetings, too few, or about the right number?"					
"Too many"	...	4.1	7.0	9.7	3.1
"About the right number"	84.1	82.4	86.6	87.1	67.2
"Too few"	9.1	13.5	5.2	3.2	28.1
"Don't know"; no answer	6.8	...	1.2	...	1.6
Total	100.0	100.0	100.0	100.0	100.0
Number	44	74	172	31	64
Question: "Are any of the paid union staff members not *doing a good job?"*					
"All doing a good job"	43.2	50.0	57.0	67.7	60.9
"Most doing a good job"	27.3	23.0	22.7	16.1	25.0
"About half and half"	4.6	9.5	5.2	3.2	3.1
"Most doing a poor job"	...	...	...	3.2	...
"All doing a poor job"	...	...	...	...	...
"Don't know"; no answer	24.9	17.5	15.1	9.8	11.0
Total	100.0	100.0	100.0	100.0	100.0
Number	44	74	172	31	64

inclined to express interest in union matters which do not concern their own shop.[3] We have also seen that older members are more willing to picket to help some other shop get organized or get a raise in pay. Table 59 illustrates the greater concern and interest of the older members in another way. Older members are considerably more likely to have read their contract and to have understood it than are newer

[3] Chapter IV.

TABLE 59. RELATIONSHIP BETWEEN LONGEVITY IN THE UNION AND INTEREST IN UNION MATTERS

Answer	Distribution of Answers by Percentage				
	Of Nonstewards, Grouped by Years in Union				Of Shop Stewards
	Under 1	1–3	4–10	Over 10	
Question: "Have you read the agreement (the contract) between your union and your company? If so, how much of it do you understand?"					
"No"	70.5	44.6	27.3	22.6	15.6
"Yes"	27.2	54.1	72.1	77.4	82.8
All of it understoood	...	12.2	16.8	19.3	32.8
Most of it understood	11.3	23.0	34.9	48.4	37.5
Some of it understood	13.6	16.2	19.2	9.7	12.5
Little or none of it understood	2.3	2.7	1.2	...	...
"Don't know"; no answer	2.3	1.3	0.6	...	1.6
Total	100.0	100.0	100.0	100.0	100.0
Number	44	74	172	31	64
Question: "How much time and money should your union put into organizing workers in places where there is no union now?"					
"A good deal"	38.6	36.5	31.4	38.7	59.4
"Some"	43.2	44.6	54.6	41.9	35.9
"Very little"	2.3	8.1	4.1	6.5	1.6
"None at all"	...	5.4	2.9	3.2	...
"Don't know"; no answer	15.9	5.4	7.0	9.7	3.1
Total	100.0	100.0	100.0	100.0	100.0
Number	44	74	172	31	64
Question: "Should your union put more time and money into unionizing these nonunion places, or should it put more into getting more and better things for the people already in the union?"					
"More into new organizational drives"	38.6	18.9	31.4	29.0	37.5
"More into working for present union members	40.9	46.0	29.7	32.3	18.7
"About same amount"	20.5	33.8	36.6	32.3	43.8
"Don't know"; no answer	...	1.3	2.3	6.4	...
Total	100.0	100.0	100.0	100.0	100.0
Number	44	74	172	31	64

members. When it comes to putting out money for union activities or sacrificing their own interests for the benefit of other workers, however, older members are not different from newer members. This also is shown in Table 59 in answers to questions about spending time and money for new organizational work. Shop stewards are somewhat more willing than rank-and-file members to put more time and money into new organizational drives.

Shop stewards naturally speak up more at union meetings than do rank-and-file members, but older members speak up no more than do members who have been in the union from one to three years. Older members, however, are more likely to feel that they get a chance to say what they think at union meetings, and thus can be said to be less critical of the union on this score. Evidence on these points is presented in Table 60.

TABLE 60. RELATIONSHIP BETWEEN LONGEVITY IN THE UNION AND SPEAKING UP AT UNION MEETINGS

	Distribution of Answers by Percentage				
	Of Nonstewards, Grouped by Years in Union				Of Shop Stewards
Answer	Under 1	1–3	4–10	Over 10	
Question: "About how often do you speak up at a union meeting?"					
"Usually several times a meeting"	2.3	5.4	3.5	3.2	34.4
"Once a meeting on the average"	...	8.2	6.4	9.7	17.2
"Only once in a while"	15.9	39.3	33.7	38.7	35.9
"Practically never"	70.5	44.7	55.2	48.4	12.5
"Don't know"; no answer	11.3	2.4	1.2	...	...
Total	100.0	100.0	100.0	100.0	100.0
Number	44	74	172	81	64
Question: "Do you get a chance to say what you think in union meetings?"					
"Yes, get a good chance"	56.8	89.2	84.3	96.8	91.6
"Get a chance if I try hard"	11.4	8.1	10.5	3.2	5.1
"No, get no chance"	4.6	...	1.2	...	3.3
"Don't know"; no answer	27.2	2.7	4.0	...	...
Total	100.0	100.0	100.0	100.0	100.0
Number	44	74	172	31	64

Shop stewards and older members do not differ from other members in their conception of the relation between the union and the employers (Table 61). Practically all members

TABLE 61. RELATIONSHIP BETWEEN LONGEVITY IN THE UNION AND ATTITUDES REGARDING UNION LEADERS AND EMPLOYERS

	Distribution of Answers by Percentage				
	Of Nonstewards, Grouped by Years in Union				Of Shop Stewards
Answer	Under 1	1–3	4–10	Over 10	
Question: "How do your union staff leaders get along with your employer?"					
"Give in too much to the employer"	...	8.1	3.5	3.2	6.2
"Just about right: they push hard enough for us, but are also fair to the employer"	90.9	82.4	91.3	87.1	85.9
"The union is sometimes unfair to the employer"	2.3	6.8	1.2	3.2	6.3
"Don't know"; no answer	6.8	2.7	4.0	6.5	1.6
Total	100.0	100.0	100.0	100.0	100.0
Number	44	74	172	31	64
Question: "Do you think you need a union to buck the employer for you, or could you do as well by yourself?"					
"Need a union"	88.6	94.6	94.2	90.4	98.4
"Could do almost as well by myself" ...	4.6	4.0	2.3	3.2	...
"Could do just as well by myself"	4.6	1.4	1.7	...	...
"Could do better by myself"	...	...	0.6	3.2	...
"Don't know"; no answer	2.2	...	1.2	3.2	1.6
Total	100.0	100.0	100.0	100.0	100.0
Number	44	74	172	31	64
Question: "Do you think your foreman is fair to the workers?"					
"Very fair most of the time"	81.8	68.9	74.4	77.4	60.9
"Sometimes fair, sometimes not fair" ...	11.4	23.0	22.1	12.9	31.3
"Hardly ever fair" ...	2.3	6.8	3.5	6.5	7.8
"Don't know"; no answer	4.5	1.3	...	3.2	...
Total	100.0	100.0	100.0	100.0	100.0
Number	44	74	172	31	64

TABLE 61 *continued*

Answer	Distribution of Answers by Percentage: Of Nonstewards, Grouped by Years in Union: Under 1	1–3	4–10	Over 10	Of Shop Stewards
Question: "Do you think the top officials and bosses of the company are fair to the workers?"					
"Very fair most of the time"	63.6	56.7	46.5	67.7	37.5
"Sometimes fair, sometimes not fair"	18.2	24.3	29.7	9.7	37.5
"Hardly ever fair"	...	4.1	2.3	...	10.9
"Don't know because I never have any contact with any of them"	18.2	14.9	21.5	22.6	12.5
No answer	...	...	...	...	1.6
Total	100.0	100.0	100.0	100.0	100.0
Number	44	74	172	31	64

are equally "sold" on the need of having a union to stand up to the employer for them, although other members are not quite so close to 100 per cent on this matter as are shop stewards. Older members do not differ significantly from other rank-and-filers in their belief that foremen and top officials of the company are fair to the workers. Shop stewards, however, are frequently critical, especially regarding the top officials, and in this respect may be said to have stronger union solidarity.

There is a large and most significant difference between old and new members in political attitudes. In the proportion voting, we would expect members who have been in the union less than one year to be about 30–35 per cent below those in the longevity groups "4–10 years" and "over 10 years" because it is such a percentage who are below voting age in the newest longevity group.[4] In fact, however, they are about 59 per cent and 69 per cent below; that is, there is

[4] On the other hand, the older longevity groups probably include more persons ineligible to vote by virtue of not being American citizens, but our point regarding differential use of the franchise can be made without bringing this factor in. Also, nonvoting is somewhat more characteristic of the aged population generally.

very little nonvoting among members who have been in the union a long time (about 23 and 13 per cent respectively for the two oldest longevity groups), but there is a large amount of nonvoting among members who have recently joined the union (about 47 per cent, if we take the proportion of those under twenty-one years of age to be 35 per cent).[5] The difference is so large as to make it likely that the union's efforts to get its members to vote can be counted a significant success.[6] Looked at from the side of the individual union member, the greater tendency to vote on the part of the older member suggests a stronger union solidarity.

In Table 62 we see other differences in political attitudes between newer and older members. Older members and shop

TABLE 62. RELATIONSHIP BETWEEN LONGEVITY IN THE UNION AND ATTITUDES TOWARD THE UNION IN POLITICS

	Proportion Saying "Yes" to Suggested Activity				
	Of Nonstewards, Grouped by Years in Union				
Suggested Political Activity of the Union	Under 1	1–3	4–10	Over 10	Of Shop Stewards
Tell members which candidates are friendly to labor	65.9	73.0	78.5	77.4	87.5
Advise members how to vote	20.5	23.0	39.5	45.2	43.8
Help to start a Labor party sometime in the future	50.0	41.9	43.0	35.5	60.9
Get union members to run for political office	63.6	68.9	70.9	64.5	75.0
Encourage union members to go to the polls	93.2	93.2	89.5	93.6	96.9
Collect a dollar from each union member to help friendly candidates	38.6	48.7	55.8	58.1	65.6
Spend union funds to get laws friendly to labor	70.5	58.1	72.7	74.2	84.4

[5] Since the survey was conducted in March, April, and May of 1949 and the election referred to was held in November 1948, many of the members under one year in the union were not members at the time of the election.

[6] Among those who voted in the presidential election, the proportion voting for Truman was about the same in all longevity groups.

stewards are more willing to have the union tell members which candidates are friendly to labor and advise members how to vote. Older members are less willing to help start a Labor party sometime in the future, and in this respect shop stewards are more like newer members in being more in favor of a Labor party. On all questions asked, shop stewards were more in favor of political action than almost every category of rank-and-file members. Older members do not differ

TABLE 63. RELATIONSHIP BETWEEN LONGEVITY IN THE UNION AND ATTITUDES REGARDING UNION FUNDS

	Distribution of Answers by Percentage				
	Of Nonstewards, Grouped by Years in Union				Of Shop Stewards
Answer	Under 1	1–3	4–10	Over 10	
Question: "Do you think union dues are too high, too low, or about right?"					
"Too high"	22.7	28.4	31.4	29.0	25.0
"About right"	72.7	67.6	67.4	58.1	73.4
"Too low"	...	...	...	...	...
"No opinion"	4.6	4.0	1.2	9.7	1.6
No answer	...	...	...	3.2	...
Total	100.0	100.0	100.0	100.0	100.0
Number	44	74	172	31	64
Question: "In addition to dues, the union sometimes asks for assessments and extra payments. Does your union ask for too many extras?"					
"Yes, too many extras"	4.6	5.4	8.7	12.9	10.9
"No, about the right amount of extras"	93.1	90.5	90.7	80.6	87.5
"Don't know"; no answer	2.3	4.1	0.6	6.5	1.6
Total	100.0	100.0	100.0	100.0	100.0
Number	44	74	172	31	64
Question: "Does your union have too many paid staff members, too few, or about the right number?"					
"Too many"	2.3	2.7	5.8	6.5	10.9
"Too few"	...	5.4	2.3	3.2	12.5
"About the right number"	68.2	75.7	73.3	61.3	64.1
"Don't know"; no answer	29.5	16.2	18.6	29.0	12.5
Total	100.0	100.0	100.0	100.0	100.0
Number	44	74	172	31	64

significantly from newer members in their willingness to get union members to run for political office, to encourage union members to go to the polls, or to spend union funds to get laws friendly to labor. They are, however, more willing to have the union collect a dollar from each member to help friendly candidates. The last fact may seem surprising in view of the fact that older members are generally more critical of union expenditures. They are less in favor of spending money for new organization, more inclined to find the dues too high and extra assessments too frequent, and more inclined to believe that the union has too many paid staff members (Table 63).[7] In view of these facts, it is all the more significant that older members are more willing than newer members to collect an extra dollar for political action. It is another strong evidence of their conviction about the need for political action.

C. Age and Sex Differences as Factors in Union Participation and Solidarity

Men are more frequent attenders of union meetings than are women, at least at all ages under fifty (Table 64).[8] Of all age and sex groups, attendance is best among men aged 30 to 49: Attendance is better for that group than for older men, and relative to women at a comparable age it is better than any other man-woman ratio. Men also speak up at meetings more than women do, and men in the age group 30 to 49 again participate most. Those who speak up least, as well as being the poorest attenders at union meetings, are young women under the age of thirty.

The lower participation in union meetings on the part of women reflects their lower interest in the union in general (Table 65). Both young men and middle-aged men say they would rather go to union meetings than to do almost any-

[7] Figures demonstrating these points are presented in Table 63, except for the question as to spending for new organizational drives. Figures on this latter point are presented in Table 59 in this chapter.

[8] We cannot draw any reliable conclusions about women over fifty, because there are not enough such workers in our sample (22 cases).

TABLE 64. RELATIONSHIP BETWEEN THE SEX AND AGE OF UNION MEMBERS AND THEIR ATTENDANCE AND PARTICIPATION AT UNION MEETINGS

	Distribution of Answers by Percentage				
	Of Men, by Age			Of Women, by Age	
Answer	Under 30	30–49	50 and Older	Under 30	30–49
Question: "About how many union meetings have you personally attended in the past year?"					
None	9.0	1.0	12.5	13.5	5.7
1–2	9.0	5.0	6.3	17.3	20.7
3–6	29.5	20.0	23.8	34.6	67.9
7–12	41.0	56.0	46.2	30.7	3.8
Over 12	10.2	15.0	10.0	3.9	...
"Don't know"; no answer	1.3	3.0	1.2	...	1.9
Total	100.0	100.0	100.0	100.0	100.0
Number	77	101	80	51	53
Question: "About how often do you speak up at a union meeting?"					
"Usually several times a meeting"	6.4	15.0	12.5	1.9	5.7
"Once a meeting on the average"	7.7	11.0	7.5	...	9.4
"Only once in a while"	35.9	42.0	32.5	25.0	35.8
"Practically never"	47.4	31.0	45.0	69.2	47.2
"Don't know"; no answer	2.6	1.0	2.5	3.9	1.9
Total	100.0	100.0	100.0	100.0	100.0
Number	77	101	80	51	53

TABLE 65. RELATIONSHIP BETWEEN THE SEX AND AGE OF UNION MEMBERS AND ATTITUDES INDICATING UNION SOLIDARITY

	Distribution of Answers by Percentage				
	Of Men, by Age			Of Women, by Age	
Answer	Under 30	30–49	50 and Older	Under 30	30–49
Question: "Would you rather go to a union meeting or would you rather spend your time doing something else like going to a good movie or playing cards?"					
"Would rather go to a union meeting than to almost anything else"	39.7	53.0	61.2	34.6	45.3
"Sometimes rather go to union meetings; sometimes something else"	37.2	30.0	22.5	34.6	30.2

TABLE 65 *continued*

Answer	Distribution of Answers by Percentage				
	Of Men, by Age			Of Women, by Age	
	Under 30	30–49	50 and Older	Under 30	30–49
"Would rather do something that I like to do"	21.8	17.0	11.3	28.9	22.6
"Don't know"; no answer	1.3	...	5.0	1.9	1.9
Total	100.0	100.0	100.0	100.0	100.0
Number	77	101	80	51	53
Question: "Do you think you need a union to buck the employer for you, or could you do as well by yourself?"					
"Need a union"	94.9	98.0	96.2	96.1	98.1
"Could do almost as well by myself"	1.3	...	1.3	3.9	...
"Could do just as well by myself"	2.6	...	...	...	1.9
"Could do better by myself"	...	1.0	1.3	...	...
"Don't know"; no answer	1.2	1.0	1.2	...	...
Total	100.0	100.0	100.0	100.0	100.0
Number	77	101	80	51	53
Question: "How much time and money should your union put into organizing workers in places where there is no union now?"					
"A great deal"	41.0	37.0	36.2	42.3	35.9
"Some"	46.2	51.0	47.5	46.1	52.8
"Very little"	2.6	3.0	3.8	3.9	1.9
"None at all"	2.6	4.0	8.8	3.9	1.9
"Don't know"; no answer	7.6	5.0	3.7	3.8	7.5
Total	100.0	100.0	100.0	100.0	100.0
Number	77	101	80	51	53
Question: "During an election year, how much money would you be willing to give in order to help candidates friendly to labor?"					
"Nothing"	20.8	21.8	17.5	29.4	22.6
$1.00	7.8	11.9	10.0	2.0	7.6
$1.01–$2.00	7.8	6.9	10.0	2.0	1.9
Over $2.00	11.7	9.9	20.0	7.8	5.7
"Something"	27.3	21.8	16.3	31.4	30.2
"Don't know"; no answer	24.6	27.7	26.2	27.4	32.0
Total	100.0	100.0	100.0	100.0	100.0
Number	77	101	80	51	53

thing else in greater proportion than do young and middle-aged women. The age differences are larger than the sex differences, however: Older people are more interested in going to union meetings than are younger people. Despite these differences in actual participation and interest in participation, overwhelming proportions in all age and sex groups feel a need for a union. There is practically no difference between the proportions of men and women, and of old and young, saying they need a union to stand up against the employer for them.

Solidarity does not extend to all aspects of union policy, however. On the question as to how much time and money should be spent on organizing workers in places where there is no union now, older people are slightly less generous than are younger people. It seems to be true here, just as in the analysis of the different longevity groups in the preceding section, that older people are more cautious about spending money. Political action is again something of an exception, for older men, at least, are more willing to make contributions to help elect candidates friendly to labor than are younger men. Women seem to be less willing to make contributions for political action than are men.

D. How Education Affects Attitudes toward the Union

Most workers have a poor educational background, and the members of Teamsters Local 688, who are employed mainly in warehouses and small food-producing factories, are no exception. But not all of them have had a poor education, as we see in Table 66. Furthermore, the future will probably see a higher educational status for all workers, for the following reasons: (1) The proportion of immigrants of peasant background among all workers is decreasing since the immigration laws of 1921 and 1924 made it difficult to enter the country. (2) Minimum educational standards in the United States have been increasing both in law and in custom. (3) Opportunities for moving out of the working class are decreasing, even if one is educated. The trend toward a higher educational level for union members is indicated in Table 66, where we see that younger workers tend to have a better educational background than older ones. Whereas 81 per cent of men over fifty years of age have not gone beyond elementary school, this is true of only 28 per cent of the men under thirty.

The central question of this section is: If the educational level of union members rises, how will that affect the internal solidarity of the union? The basis of our prediction is limited to how the more educated members now feel. This has two weaknesses for predictive purposes: (1) Other factors and events besides the rising educational level will influence union solidarity, and these are not considered in this chapter. (2) When most members of a union are educated, the personality characteristics of the educated members will have a wider range than they now have, when only a few members are educated. These personality characteristics will also influence union solidarity, and we are saying that they will change – on the average – as the proportion of educated members rises.

TABLE 66. EDUCATIONAL BACKGROUND OF UNION MEMBERS, ACCORDING TO SEX AND AGE

Highest Educational Level Achieved	Percentage of All Members	Percentage of Men, by Age			Percentage of Women, by Age		
		Under 30	30–49	50 and Older	Under 30	30–49	50 and Older
Through 6th grade	9.7	...	7.0	32.5	1.9	3.8	9.1
7th or 8th grade	39.8	28.2	47.0	48.7	21.2	37.7	68.2
Some high school	28.6	43.6	23.0	8.8	42.3	37.7	18.2
Graduation from high school	16.6	24.3	19.0	5.0	23.1	18.9	4.5
Some college	4.1	2.6	3.0	3.7	11.5	1.9	...
No answer	1.2	1.3	1.0	1.3	...	...	...
Total	100.0	100.0	100.0	100.0	100.0	100.0	100.0
Number	392 *	77	101	80	51	53	23

* The total number includes seven persons for whom information on age is lacking.

Judging from our representative sample, 4.1 per cent of the members of Local 688 have gone to college (although practically none of these have graduated). Adding these to the 16.6 per cent who have graduated from high school but have not gone to college, we get our category of educated members. At the other end, almost half (49.5 per cent) of the members have had only an elementary school education

TABLE 67. RELATIONSHIP BETWEEN THE EDUCATIONAL LEVEL OF UNION MEMBERS AND ATTITUDES INDICATING UNION SOLIDARITY

Answer	Percentage of Members Giving Indicated Answer, According to Educational Group		
	Through 8th Grade or Less	Some High School	High School Graduation or Some College
Question: "Do you think you need a union to buck the employer for you, or could you do as well by yourself?"			
"Need a union"	94.3	93.8	90.3
"Could do almost as well by myself"	2.1	2.6	6.1
"Could do just as well by myself"	1.5	1.8	1.2
"Could do better by myself"	0.5	0.9	1.2
"Don't know"; no answer	1.6	0.9	1.2
Total	100.0	100.0	100.0
Number	197	113	82
Question: "What do you think of bonuses, piecework pay, and other rewards for harder work?"			
"Like them"	38.1	37.2	53.7
"Don't like them"	43.2	44.2	32.9
"Don't care either way"	14.2	16.8	9.8
"Don't know"; no answer	4.5	1.8	3.6
Total	100.0	100.0	100.0
Number	197	113	82
Question: "How much time and money should your union put into organizing workers in places where there is no union now?"			
"A great deal"	33.0	40.7	46.3
"Some"	51.8	49.6	41.5
"Very little"	2.0	0.9	3.7
"None at all"	2.6	3.5	3.7
"Don't know"; no answer	10.6	5.3	4.8
Total	100.0	100.0	100.0
Number	197	113	82

or less. Our first major conclusion is that there is very little difference between the well educated and the poorly educated groups in the general feeling that a union is necessary (Table 67).

In the more specific attitudes by which union leaders measure solidarity, however, there are significant differences. On the one hand, the better educated members are somewhat more likely to reject certain basic union principles, if they feel that the latter hold them down. For example, 53.7 per cent of the better educated members say they like piecework pay and other incentives for harder work, as compared to only 37 or 38 per cent of the less well educated members. On the other hand, the better educated members are somewhat more likely to favor measures that strengthen the whole union, and thereby help them as well as other members. For example, 46.3 per cent of them say that a great deal of time and money should be spent by the union in new organization, as compared to 33.0 per cent of the least well educated group.

As might be expected, the better educated members of the union are more inclined to think they have a chance to become foremen or employers themselves someday (Table 68). However, the difference between them and the less well educated members of the union is not great. Only 4.9 per cent of the better educated members say they have a good chance (as compared to 2.0 per cent of the poorly educated), and 23.2 per cent say they have a fair chance (as compared to 14.1 per cent of the poorly educated). Thus an expectation of rising out of the ranks of ordinary workers is not likely to affect the union loyalty of too many more of the educated members than of the uneducated members. If the educated members have any more ambition, it does not extend to their becoming union officers or staff members: Only 11 per cent say they have ever thought of becoming union leaders, and this is the same proportion as among the poorly educated. Insofar as ambition to become a union leader helps to make for success in union leadership, no more can be ex-

TABLE 68. RELATIONSHIP BETWEEN THE EDUCATIONAL LEVEL OF UNION MEMBERS AND THEIR AMBITION AND BELIEF IN OPPORTUNITY

Answer	Distribution of Answers by Percentage, According to Educational Group: Through 8th Grade or Less	Some High School	High School Graduation or Some College
Question: "Have you ever thought of trying to become a union officer or staff member?"			
"Yes, often"	4.6	6.2	3.7
"Yes, occasionally"	6.6	15.0	7.3
"No, never"	87.3	77.9	89.0
"Don't know"; no answer	1.5	0.9	. . .
Total	100.0	100.0	100.0
Number	197	113	82
Question: "What chance do you think you have for getting ahead and becoming a foreman or shop owner yourself someday?"			
"No chance at all"	55.9	43.4	39.0
"Very small chance"	23.9	23.0	29.3
"Fair chance"	14.1	18.6	23.2
"Good chance"	2.0	6.2	4.9
"Don't know"; no answer	4.1	8.8	3.6
Total	100.0	100.0	100.0
Number	197	113	82

pected from the well-educated members than from the poorly educated.

The lack of ambition to become union leaders on the part of most of the educated members is reflected in the fact that they do not speak up at union meetings any more than do the poorly educated members (if anything they speak up somewhat less). Table 69 also shows that while the educated members are somewhat more inclined to want important matters to be decided by the rank and file rather than by the union's director, they are no more concerned that the union be democratic than are the poorly educated members.

In other ways, too, the well-educated members are only slightly more inclined to be critical than are the poorly educated. While 43.9 per cent of the high education group say the union is run very well, 47.0 per cent of the low education

TABLE 69. RELATIONSHIP BETWEEN THE EDUCATIONAL LEVEL OF UNION MEMBERS AND THEIR DESIRE FOR PARTICIPATION IN UNION ACTIVITIES

Answer	Distribution of Answers by Percentage, According to Educational Group		
	Through 8th Grade or Less	Some High School	High School Graduation or Some College
Question: "About how often do you speak up at a union meeting?"			
"Usually several times a meeting"	7.6	11.5	8.5
"Once a meeting on the average"	8.1	7.1	8.5
"Only once in a while"	35.5	40.7	23.2
"Practically never"	47.2	38.9	54.9
"Don't know"; no answer	1.6	1.8	4.9
Total	100.0	100.0	100.0
Number	197	113	82
Question: "Would you rather have important matters affecting the union be decided by the union director, by the stewards' council, or by the rank-and-file members?"			
"By the union director"	9.1	6.2	1.2
"By the stewards' council"	23.9	23.0	23.2
"By the rank-and-file members"	61.4	66.4	74.4
"Don't know"; no answer	5.6	4.4	1.2
Total	100.0	100.0	100.0
Number	197	113	82
Question: "Is it more important that the top leaders get what the members want and need than it is that the union be democratic, or is it more important for the union to be democratic?"			
"More important that the union get what members want and need"	32.0	29.2	36.6
"More important that the union be democratic"	53.8	53.1	53.7
"Don't know"	13.7	17.7	7.3
No answer	0.5	...	2.4
Total	100.0	100.0	100.0
Number	197	113	82

group express this opinion (Table 70). Similarly, while 50.0 per cent of the high education group say that all of the paid union staff members are doing a good job, 56.1 per cent of the lower education group express this opinion.

A final set of attitudes that we shall relate to education are those toward the role of the union in politics (Table 71).

TABLE 70. RELATIONSHIP BETWEEN THE EDUCATIONAL LEVEL OF UNION MEMBERS AND THEIR OPINIONS OF HOW THE UNION IS RUN

Answer	Distribution of Answers by Percentage, According to Educational Group		
	Through 8th Grade or Less	Some High School	High School Graduation or Some College
Question: "In general, what do you think of the way your union is run?"			
"It is run very well"	47.0	48.7	43.9
"It is run fairly well"	44.4	44.2	43.9
"It is not run so well"	4.5	2.7	2.4
"It is run very poorly"	2.5	3.5	7.3
"Don't know"; no answer	1.6	0.9	2.5
Total	100.0	100.0	100.0
Number	197	113	82
Question: "Are any of the paid union staff members not doing a good job?"			
"All doing a good job"	56.1	56.7	50.0
"Most doing a good job"	21.7	23.9	24.4
"About half and half"	6.6	4.4	6.1
"Most doing a poor job"	1.0	...	...
"All doing a poor job"	...	...	...
"Don't know"; no answer	14.6	15.0	19.5
Total	100.0	100.0	100.0
Number	197	113	82

Well-educated members are slightly more willing to have the union spend time and money in getting candidates friendly to labor elected to public office. But, if anything, they are slightly less willing to have the union help start a Labor party in the future.

In sum, there is little difference between well-educated and less well educated members of the union. In general union solidarity they are the same. In being willing to have the union spend time and money for new organization and politics, the better educated are slightly more in agreement with modern union aims than the poorly educated, but they give slightly less support to the union's fight against piecework pay or other kinds of incentives. Although a somewhat larger proportion of the well-educated would allocate ultimate union control to the rank and file, they are really no

TABLE 71. RELATIONSHIP BETWEEN THE EDUCATIONAL LEVEL OF UNION MEMBERS AND THEIR ATTITUDES TOWARD THE UNION'S ENGAGING IN POLITICS

Answer	Distribution of Answers by Percentage, According to Educational Group		
	Through 8th Grade or Less	Some High School	High School Graduation or Some College
Question: "How much time and money should your union put into getting candidates elected to public office who are friendly to labor?"			
"A great deal"	29.4	27.4	37.8
"Some"	49.3	51.3	43.9
"Very little"	9.1	6.2	7.3
"None at all"	5.6	8.9	8.5
"Don't know"; no answer	6.6	6.2	2.5
Total	100.0	100.0	100.0
Number	197	113	82
Question: "Should the union help to start a Labor party sometime in the future?"			
"Yes"	45.7	44.2	43.9
"No"	43.7	40.7	51.2
"Don't know"; no answer	10.6	15.1	4.9
Total	100.0	100.0	100.0
Number	197	113	82

more concerned with democracy in the union. They are no more ambitious to become union leaders, although a slightly larger proportion of them think they have a good chance to become foremen or bosses. They do not speak up at union meetings to any greater extent, and they are only slightly more critical of union leaders and of their management of the union.

E. Religion and Attitudes toward the Union

The church is, in a sense, a rival of the union for the time and loyalty of the members. Americans of the lower income groups usually belong to few or no organizations other than a church and/or a union. It is doubtful, however, that the average worker sees any conflict between the two organizations, since he considers them to be in completely different spheres of his life. Nevertheless, the various denominations make different demands on the time and loyalty of their members and in other ways promote different attitudes toward unions. This is increasingly true as some denominations are beginning to take part in union activities.

Unfortunately, our sample is not large enough to permit a comparison of all denominations. We shall be obliged to group all churchgoing Protestants together, to combine nonchurchgoers of both Protestant and Catholic backgrounds, and to ignore Jews (since there are only five Jews in the sample). It is also deemed wise not to include Negroes, who in our sample are all Protestant churchgoers, because it is desired to get a religious differential uninfluenced by the race differential.

There are no great differences among the religious groups in union meeting attendance or participation (Table 72). The nonchurchgoers are slightly underrepresented in the group that attend more than twelve meetings a year — these are mostly the shop stewards. For regular attendance (seven to twelve meetings a year), the Catholic churchgoers have the best record. In regard to speaking up at union meetings, there are no significant differences among the religious groups.

Nor is there any evidence of differences among them in union solidarity. The answers to questions regarding the general necessity of a union and the need of feeling secure against arbitrary action by the employer are distributed in almost exactly the same way for all religious groups. In other words, there is nothing in this survey that would indicate that Catholics are at all different from Protestants, or churchgoers from nonchurchgoers, in their attitudes regarding the importance of a union. The only religious difference between members, mentioned in Chapter V, is that nonchurchgoers are the least prejudiced against minority groups and Protestant churchgoers the most prejudiced.

TABLE 72. RELATIONSHIP BETWEEN THE RELIGIOUS PREFERENCES OF UNION MEMBERS AND MEASURES OF UNION PARTICIPATION AND SOLIDARITY

Answer	Distribution of Answers by Percentage, According to Religious Preference		
	Catholic Churchgoers	Protestant Churchgoers	Nonchurchgoers of Catholic or Protestant Background
Question: "About how many union meetings have you personally attended in the past year?"			
None	8.9	7.5	7.0
1–2	5.9	9.8	9.9
3–6	19.3	25.6	25.3
7–12	54.8	44.3	47.9
Over 12	10.4	12.8	8.5
No answer	0.7	...	1.4
Total	100.0	100.0	100.0
Number	135	133	71
Question: "About how often do you speak up at a union meeting?"			
"Usually several times a meeting"	8.9	9.0	11.3
"Once a meeting on the average"	7.4	10.5	7.0
"Only once in a while"	31.9	31.6	32.4
"Practically never"	48.9	47.4	46.5
"Don't know"; no answer	2.9	1.5	2.8
Total	100.0	100.0	100.0
Number	135	133	71
Question: "Do you think you need a union to buck the employer for you, or could you do as well by yourself?"			
"Need a union"	96.3	95.5	95.8
"Could do almost as well by myself"	3.0	1.5	1.4
"Could do just as well by myself"	...	2.3	1.4
"Could do better by myself"	0.7	0.7	...
"Don't know"; no answer	...	...	1.4
Total	100.0	100.0	100.0
Number	135	133	71
Question: "Since you are a member of a union, do you feel that your boss can't push you around as much as he might want to?"			
"Yes, he can't push me around"	73.3	73.3	70.4
"No, the union hardly helps at all"	5.2	3.8	5.6
"The union helps some, but not completely"	19.3	21.3	21.2
"Don't know"; no answer	2.2	1.6	2.8
Total	100.0	100.0	100.0
Number	135	133	71

F. Summary

1. Older members differ from newer members in thinking that there are too many union meetings, in being most concerned about matters which do not concern their own shop, in having read and understood their contract, in being more willing to picket, in being less willing for the union to spend time and money in new organizational drives, in being more active and interested in politics (but less in favor of such a political activity as starting a new Labor party), and in being less willing to spend union money (except for political action). Older members do *not* differ from newer members in their general evaluation of the way the union is run, in their attitudes as to whether staff members are doing a good job, in the amount of speaking up at union meetings, or in their conception of the relation between employers and the union. In general, older members show more union solidarity (except when that involves spending money) but are not necessarily less critical of certain specific union activities.

2. Shop stewards differ from most other members in thinking that there are too few union meetings, in believing that more time and money should be put into new organizational drives, and in being less inclined to think employers are fair. In general, shop stewards exhibit more union solidarity than do other members.

3. Men attend union meetings, and speak up at them, more frequently than do women. They also show other evidences of greater participation. Young people show fewer signs of union solidarity than do members of more mature age, except that they are more willing to contribute money for union purposes than are old members.

4. Taken in the balance, there is little evidence of differences in union solidarity between the better educated and the poorly educated members. Better educated members are more in favor of putting time and money into new organizational drives and into political action, but also are more in favor of incentive pay (which union leaders believe breaks down solidarity). They are more likely to think they have a

chance of becoming foremen or shop owners, and they have no more ambition than the poorly educated to become union officers. Also they do not speak up at union meetings any more frequently. On the other hand, they are somewhat more in favor of rank-and-file control of the union. They do not differ in their evaluation of the union management or of the staff members.

5. The religious affiliation of the members makes little difference in their participation in union activities or in general union solidarity. Only in attitudes toward minority groups were significant differences among religious groups discovered in this survey (nonchurchgoers were the least prejudiced and Protestant churchgoers the most prejudiced).

CHAPTER VIII

Conclusions: Practical and Theoretical

Summaries at the end of Chapters III through VII report the specific findings of the survey. In this brief chapter our purpose is to translate some of these findings from descriptive terms into practical and theoretical terms. By practical conclusions we mean those that should be useful to union leaders, particularly those of Local 688. By theoretical conclusions we mean those that should have an interest for students of human relations generally.

This study of the attitudes of union members toward their union was conducted by the method of the questionnaire survey[1] and is subject to the limitations of that method. At some points in this study it has become apparent that a longer and more unstructured interview, which would probe deeper into the respondents' unconscious, would have provided more important information. At certain other points in the study it has seemed that observation of the activities of union members by an observer participating in the activities would have better provided the information we sought. But these methods were not feasible, and the questionnaire survey had to be adapted to substitute for them. The method proved to be highly satisfactory in most instances, and most of the data are believed to be highly reliable. Where the information is weak, we have so indicated in the body of the report.

[1] See Chapter II of this book; also Arnold M. Rose, "Attitude Measurement and the Questionnaire Survey," *Scientific Monthly*, LXVIII (February 1949), 97–101.

The method does, however, place certain limitations on the practical and theoretical value of the study. The descriptive character of most findings indicates what the union is at present, not so much what it might become. Statements about causal relationships have had to be made most tentatively. Nevertheless, the descriptive finding, for example, that there is a strong loyalty to the principle of unionism and to this particular union despite criticisms of its specific policies and practices is one that has great practical and theoretical value. The union leader can be sure that he has a firm foundation to build on even if part of his superstructure is flimsy, and the social psychologist can note the existence of conflicts of attitudes when the attitudes are at two different levels. Further, the union leader can know in what directions he may most safely experiment, and the social psychologist will have an opportunity to observe the effects of these experiments in social change. Too, the social historian can observe that, at this time, the overwhelming majority of workers are in favor of the *principle* of unionism even if there is dissatisfaction with the management of specific unions. It is with these understandings that the following conclusions are reported.

A. Practical Conclusions

1. The strong loyalty to the union is closely associated with two variables: (*a*) the success that the union has in achieving its goals of increasing the workers' income, security, and job satisfaction; (*b*) the amount of participation in union activities the rank-and-file members engage in. The first variable is something that union leaders naturally try to maximize, but it is limited by such uncontrollable factors as the business cycle and the relative strength of union and management. The second variable is much less obvious; some union leaders even consider rank-and-file participation a hindrance to their own efforts. But it may keep the union together in times of adversity, when the union is not able to achieve its goals. Encouraging the members to attend meet-

ings, to speak up, to picket, to help formulate contract proposals, and so on, would definitely seem to strengthen the members' loyalty to the union.

2. The above point is especially true if there is a significant portion of the members that want to participate. A frustrated desire to participate is worse for union loyalty than no desire to participate. The best way to determine how much interest in union participation there is would be to offer a favorable opportunity and count the number of members who turn out. It cannot be judged *a priori* since the survey disclosed that even some aged members and members who could not speak good English wanted to participate.

3. Since the attitude of the member's family toward the union is closely associated with the member's own attitude, it is probably worth while for the union to encourage some kinds of union participation by the members' families. There is fairly strong support for inviting spouses to regular union meetings, and this might serve as a minimum involvement. If this is deemed inadvisable, the setting up of wives' auxiliaries might serve the same function and also have other advantages for the union.

4. Union solidarity does not, at the present time at least, mean antagonism to employers. Union members would probably resent a union action which they considered to be unfair to the employer.

5. Partly because they have this sense of fairness, union members realize that there may be a limit beyond which employers cannot increase wages and still remain in business. They would not deem it a failure of the union if it did not press for wage increases that might jeopardize the existence of the business.

6. The union members are enthusiastic about the newer, supplementary functions of unions, such as extending security and providing recreational affairs. There is evidence that a majority now consider these functions more important than the traditional ones of getting higher wages and shorter hours. Thus if circumstances surrounding collective bargain-

ing should shift, the members are increasingly ready to accept a shifted emphasis to the supplementary functions. Even though only a small proportion of the membership makes use of the union as a source of information (regarding the law and government benefits, for example) most of the members appreciate having this information available.

7. There is a demand for more systematic notification of members as to when meetings will be held. Some members specify that they would favor having a regular meeting time. There is little criticism of the time or frequency of meetings. Older members are especially opposed to increasing the number of meetings. Most of the members favor meetings of shop size, rather than of the crew size recommended by experts.

8. The union has not completely solved the problem of communicating to its members the reasons for major policies and actions. This may be partly due to the fact that about 20 per cent of the members have not been getting the union newspaper and that another group, only slightly smaller, do not read the front page even though they do get the paper. It would probably be a wise procedure to explain all *major* policies and actions orally in union meetings, for at least two reasons: (1) The study has shown that, in several specific respects, knowledge of union policies and achievements is related to favorable attitudes toward the union and to union solidarity. (2) The study has shown that the more the member knows about the reasons for the union's actions and about the limitations on the leader's power, the less he is likely to believe the union undemocratic.

9. While member support for the union is high generally, there are a few shops in which it is not so high. This variation should be recognized as operating in all situations.

10. Being forced to join the union because the company has a union shop is not a major deterrent to union solidarity.

11. The major criticisms of the staff members is that they are too radical and too bossy, and that there are too many "outsiders" among them.

12. The major criticism of the handling of union activities is directed at the organization of new shops. Yet this is regarded as a very important function.

13. Educated members of the union, on the whole, present neither a problem of morale nor a source of eager potential leaders. They are much like other members except for a larger amount of individuality, which leads them, in greater proportion, to favor incentive pay and to recognize that they have a better chance of rising in the industrial scale. As union members rise in educational status, unions will have to pay increasing attention to these particular attitudes, and attempt to rechannel them toward union goals.

14. Members are not in favor of an increase in dues, even to support the activities they approve. The only exception is that a bare majority are willing to contribute an extra dollar for political activity during election years. Older members are more opposed to an increase in dues, despite their stronger support of union functions. Also, those who know less about union activities are more likely to consider the dues high. A more thorough explanation of union, especially staff, functions would probably reduce some opposition to high dues.

15. Union loyalties of the members are attached to the local union, not to the international – in the case of this union. Thus there was little opposition to the shift from CIO to AF of L.

16. The inauguration of a free employment service would be a most popular extra service for the union to perform. However, since the real complaint is against the high cost of the private employment service, it might be more in accord with the public welfare for the union to work through political channels for an improved public employment service and for legislation regulating the private employment agency. The projected new home for the union, with recreational facilities, would be popular too, but the large extra expense would not be borne willingly.

17. The recommendations for the *Midwest Labor World*

would be to have a more complete coverage in "News from the Shops" and to have more educational articles.

18. The proportion saying they want an educational course now is 9.2 per cent. Many of these have already taken a course, indicating that it is the same small group that would continue to sign up for new course offerings. Some of the demand is for specialized technical courses, which the union could not provide but which public technical schools do now offer. The most popular general course is one on labor economics and collective bargaining. A course on minority groups would not be very popular and would reach mainly those who are already ethnically liberal. There is more of a future for workers' education as a "filler" in general meetings than as separate courses. Discussions, lectures, and films, in that order, would be popular as such fillers.

19. While there is strong anti-Negro prejudice in general, most white members are willing to recognize Negro rights in the union. There is practically no opposition to the union's prominority policy, and there is good evidence that this policy has changed the conscious attitudes of a small minority of its members. It has possibly made some of the others more ethnically liberal also, in the strictly union situation, but these would not consider that their feelings had changed. Although evidence is not complete from this survey, it would seem that emphasis on the economic and legal *rights* of Negro members is one of the most effective ways in which the union can change the ethnic attitudes of its white members.

20. Only a small minority of the members would restrict the rights or privileges of Jews. But a sizable proportion adhere to false stereotypes about Jews.

21. In ethnic attitudes, clerical workers, educated members, and nonchurchgoers are more liberal than other groups. This fact might be made use of in planning future activities under the union's prominority policy.

22. The great majority of the members regard the strike as a union technique to be used when needed. Only a few

would have it used often to prove power, and not many more would prohibit its use completely.

23. Reading and understanding the contract between union and employer are major prerequisites to approving it. This is additional evidence that adequate communication between union leaders and members is an important ingredient in union solidarity. A significant proportion of union members have never read their contract, and some who have read it do not understand it.

24. The great majority of members see the union as an instrument for achieving common goals. Few think of it as an avenue to leadership or personal promotion. The few who would like to be union officials are *not* the ones who believe the avenues to promotion on the job are blocked. They are thus less likely to be motivated by frustration, and more by general interest.

25. Past efforts to get members to vote in political elections and to support candidates friendly to labor have apparently been attended by marked success. In advising members how to vote, the union must avoid giving the impression that it is dictating to them, since that would be regarded as a violation of democratic rights. Stressing the candidates' attitudes on issues important to working people (both labor issues and general issues) is probably the most effective approach.

B. Theoretical Conclusions

There is a philosophic difference among social scientists regarding whether or not the conclusions derived from a study of one social group, and generalized into abstract terms, are applicable to another social group. Our position is that they are not automatically so, no matter how abstract, conceptualized, and devoid of specific content the terminology.[2] Each group has a unique history and a unique configu-

[2] For a statement of our methodological position see Arnold M. Rose, "The Selection of Problems for Research," *American Journal of Sociology*, LIV (November 1948), 219–227, and "Generalizations in the Social Sciences," to be published.

ration of personalities and interpersonal relationships, which influence observations made on it. No matter how abstract the terminology, generalizations drawn from these observations are descriptive necessarily of only the one social group at a specific period in its history. Nevertheless, within our partially homogeneous culture, groups with the same social function have a somewhat similar history and a somewhat similar configuration of relationships among their members. To the extent that this similarity exists between our union and other unions or other groups which are not unions, the generalizations drawn in our survey are applicable to other groups. Each reader will have to judge for himself the probable similarity between Teamsters Local 688 and other social groups he may have in mind if he wishes to get the full value of our conclusions.

There are certain conclusions, however, where the issue of generalizability does not apply. These refer to the diversity of human behavior, not its similarity. These tell us that human beings *can* act in a certain way, not that they *are likely* to act in this way. Such conclusions are frequently provided us by anthropology, and are valuable because they extend the limits of our thinking even if they do not allow us to make predictions. We shall start our list of conclusions with some of this type.

1. People can have loyalty to two (or more) groups or two sets of values, even when those groups or values are in conflict. In concrete terms, loyalty to the union does not mean disloyalty to the employer. In this study we have not examined the concrete psychological mechanisms by means of which this dual loyalty can occur, but this would be a worth-while subject for further research.

2. It is possible to have diverse attitudes toward the same social object. More concretely, it is possible to have strong loyalty to a union and still be highly critical of some aspects of its structure or operations. Another way to state the conclusion is to say that one can have different attitudes toward a principle and toward an organization effectuating the prin-

ciple. In the case of this union, the members have a higher degree of loyalty to the principle of unionism than to the specific organization of the union. This conclusion seems fairly obvious; yet many people—including many public opinion pollsters—forget about it. It applies to specific union policies as well as to the union itself. Take the issue of job seniority, for example. A young worker may feel it is a good thing because it gives him security for his old age and because he recognizes that his older co-workers have fewer chances than he of getting another job. On the other hand, he may at the same time resent it when it throws him out of work and keeps people on the job who are less able or less ambitious.

Now we shall turn to some conclusions which allow prediction of probable behavior, but which are culturally limited.

3. Union leaders and union experiences are effective teachers of social attitudes, especially on matters associated with jobs. Since so much of social life is connected, closely or remotely, with earning a livelihood, labor leaders have a powerful influence on working people. This is all the more important because of the fact that most workers have few direct contacts with organizations or formal leaders outside of unions (the sole significant exception being the church and religious leaders).

4. The process of social learning requires, among other things, (*a*) a personal situation conducive to learning (this may be called a "need" or "desire" to learn, if it is recognized that the need is socially created and not biological), and (*b*) communication between the teaching influence and the learner. Under existing cultural conditions the personal situation of the worker is highly conducive to learning about most matters connected with his job. This is probably because he feels a strong sense of insecurity regarding the permanence of his job and because he knows he has very little control over the conditions of his employment. The second requirement mentioned—communication—is not al-

ways present, however: Union leaders are not always good articulators, and they do not always understand the many requirements for effective communication. Thus there are many blocks to communication within a union, which prevents the satisfaction and the loyalty of the rank-and-file workers from reaching a maximum. To the extent that the communication process is stepped up—through such things as increasing the members' participation in union meetings, using workers' education, and providing a union newspaper—the effectiveness of the learning process will increase, as will union solidarity.

5. The union is least effective in changing the attitudes of its members when the changes would be contrary to the basic values or deep-seated culture patterns of the society as a whole. This is illustrated by the relative opposition to or ineffectiveness of efforts to tell members how to vote or to have social relations with Negroes. However, the concept of unionism itself is so accepted by working people that being *forced* to join a union does not result in diminished loyalty to it, even though it goes against the American value of voluntary choice.

6. Social learning developed in one context is not necessarily transferred to other comparable contexts, at least when external social pressures work against that transfer. That is, changes in attitudes toward minorities taught for the union or work situation are not necessarily transferred to the home or school situation.

7. Attitudes arising out of past experience with an organization result in invidious comparisons between past and present, while at the same time the long experience results in a deeper loyalty to the organization. In other words, older members tend to be more critical of union conditions that do not seem to be as good as they used to be, yet they have had more participation and communication within the union so that their basic loyalty is stronger.

8. If there is a basic need for an organization, and yet its original activities are no longer so possible to keep up, mem-

bers will attach themselves to new activities which fit into the framework of their needs.

9. Despite differential demands on the time and loyalty of Catholic and Protestant churchgoers and nonchurchgoers, there is practically no difference between these groups with respect to their attendance at union meetings and their loyalty to the union. Not only does this mean that there is no conflict between these two institutions in the minds of their common members, but also that people do not consider that they have a certain amount of time (within limits) to spend outside the home or job. Rather, they seem to consider each demand on their time and loyalty in terms of its intrinsic merits.

10. Making contributions to or sacrifices for an organization tends to increase loyalty to it. This principle has been enunciated by Kurt Lewin[3] and our findings corroborate it.

[3] *Resolving Social Conflicts* (New York: Harper, 1948), p. 199.

APPENDIX I

Suggestions for the Union's Newspaper

An open-ended question, referring to the union's newspaper, asked: "Is there anything you would like to see in the *Midwest Labor World* which is not there now?" Of the 43 persons answering, 13 requested more news about their own shop. The feature "News from the Shops" is the most popular part of the newspaper, but apparently many of the shops are not represented each week. Among the several general suggestions about the newspaper we find the following: "Should be larger." "Too one-sided." "Too gossipy." Requests for specific items of news included:

	Number of times requested
Financial report of the union	4
Better shop-sports coverage	4
More educational articles (nonunion)	3
Educational column (on union matters)	2
Letter column (letters from members)	2
Comic strips	2
More description of LHI	2
Articles on union's history for new members	1
More news of events in Washington	1
Articles on kinds of work done in various shops	1
Article on Taft-Hartley Act	1
Articles on employment opportunities	1
Articles on other unions in St. Louis	1
Explanation of change in International affiliation	1
Better explanation of union policy	1
Article on the union and the wage scale	1
Column on sewing news and patterns	1

It may be noted that many of the specific requests fall under the heading of workers' education.

APPENDIX II

The Schedule and Its Weaknesses

Although the schedule used in this survey had the benefit of a pretest and of criticism from union leaders and social scientists, and although it was found to be understood in almost its entirety by the interviewed workers, there are nevertheless some weaknesses in it that should be pointed out for the benefit of those who contemplate repeating this study in another union. The schedule was designed to be filled out by an interviewer rather than by the respondent himself, so that some of the apparently difficult questions (like numbers 5 and 6) are not really difficult after the interviewing procedure on them has been explained to the interviewer.

But question 9 is an example of the few questions that proved to be confusing to some workers. It asks, "What do you think of bonuses, piecework pay, and other rewards for harder work?" The question was deliberately framed to have three referents, so that two could be specific and the other one general. It was felt that the general referent ("rewards for harder work") could not be understood without the specific referents ("bonuses," "piecework pay") and that the specific ones would not by themselves convey the intent of the question. These facts came out in the pretest, and they seemed to hold up in the final questioning. The difficulty was that some of the workers could think of bonuses only in terms of equal Christmas bonuses for everyone, and these are not rewards for harder work but rather gifts to all workers, regardless of their output. Some respondents answered the question by saying that they were against "rewards for harder work" but in favor of Christmas bonuses. While these were edited to have a negative answer, the question remains faulty, and the possibility exists that there are still too many positive answers.

Question 26 proved difficult for some respondents: "What do you think are the *main things* your union should work for right now, either through collective bargaining or through social action in the community?" The purpose of the latter half of the question was to increase the range of possibilities in the minds of the respondents (since question 5 is a similar question which elicits only spontaneous responses). Because of the difficulty of the question, it might be better to use just the first half of the question, and then allow the interviewer to use the second half if he finds the respondent thinking in the too narrow terms of the collective bargaining functions of the union.

Question 22 was not immediately clear to some respondents: "Do union problems which do *not* concern your shop interest you? (If asked 'What do you mean?' say, 'Like getting more members, labor politics')." However, good interviewers had little difficulty in getting the meaning across by using the instruction in the parentheses.

Question 117, "Have any of your family ever belonged to a union?" confused some respondents because they did not know whether to include collateral relatives or only those in the immediate family. The answers in terms of collateral relatives are not reliable.

Questions 59 and 60, which refer to the "place where you work," were not clear for some because they did not know whether their department or their company was being referred to. Probably this confusion did not hurt the answers since either choice would be satisfactory to meet the intent of the question.

Question 119 reads, "What chance do you think you would have for getting ahead and becoming a foreman or shop owner yourself someday?" The use of two referents ("foreman" and "shop owner") is bad because a foreman is not necessarily a higher-status position. A foreman does not get the benefits of union activity, and his pay is usually not greatly above that of the ordinary worker. Referring to "small shop owner" would be preferable.

Reversing the order of the checklists in half of the schedules is a desirable practice, in order to see if the order of the checklist items affects choice. We did this with a small proportion of the schedules in our survey, and there was no evidence that choice was thereby influenced. However, we did not carefully match the two groups of respondents getting the two kinds of schedules, and our results are therefore not conclusive.

One can think of other questions which it would be desirable to have in a schedule for a study of this sort. A feasible schedule has natural limits of length that one must adhere to, and thus one must forgo the satisfaction of some of his scientific interests. One question, however, it grieved us particularly to leave out, and that was one on the fellowship satisfactions given to the workers by association in the union. This could, of course, be a study by itself.

Questions 102 and 119, on *ambition* to become a union officer and on the *possibility* of becoming a foreman or shop owner, would have been more useful if they had been supplemented by the complementary questions on the *possibility* of becoming a union officer and *ambition* to become a foreman or shop owner. Another question which it would have been valuable to include is one on the worker's consciousness of being unskilled and hence easily replaceable by the employer. The objective fact of being unskilled the workers in this union share with most other industrial workers, and a consciousness of the implication of this fact for their job security is probably a basis of loyalty to the union.

The complete schedule, exactly as used in this survey, is reproduced on the following pages. The reader can see that it consists of 129 questions, 125 of which are to be answered by the respondent and 4 by the interviewer. The mimeographed schedule was 13 pages long.

Not a matter of question selection, but of presentation, was our decision to report percentages to one decimal place. While it is recognized that accuracy is not so great as to justify referring to fractions of a per cent, the figures were presented this way because sometimes misleading differences seem to appear if decimals are dropped. In the text, no differences are referred to unless they are statistically significant.

The Schedule

1. How many people in your shop are interested in union activities?
   1______Most of them 2______About half of them 3______Very few of them
2. How many speak up at meetings?
   1______Most of them 2______About half of them 3______Very few of them
3. In general, what do you think of the way your union is run?
   1______It is run very well
   2______It is run fairly well
   3______It is not run so well
   4______It is run very poorly
4. What is the reason for your answer?____________________
   ____
   ____
5. What do you consider to be the purposes of your union? (What is a union for?)
   (How accomplished?)
   a.____________________ _______________
   b.____________________ _______________
   c.____________________ _______________
   d.____________________ _______________
   e.____________________ _______________
   Is that all? Any other purposes? (Do *not* hint at purposes.)
6. How well do you think your union does each of these things?
   1. Unusually well 2. Pretty well 3. Average 4. Fairly poorly 5. Not at all
   (Re-read each of the purposes given, and put the number of the answer in the space opposite the purpose.)
7. How do your union staff leaders get along with your employer?
   1______Give in too much to the employer. (Why?____________________)
   2______Just about right: They push hard enough for us, but are also fair to the employer.
   3______The union is sometimes unfair to the employer (in what ways?______
   ____
   ____)
8. Do you think you need a union to buck the employer for you, or could you do as well by yourself?
   1______Need a union
   2______Could do *almost as well* by myself
   3______Could do *just as well* by myself
   4______Could do better by myself
9. What do you think of bonuses, piecework pay, and other rewards for harder work?
   1______Like them
   2______Don't like them
   3______Don't care either way
10. Do you think your foreman is fair to the workers? (Floorwalker; boss immediately above worker)
    1______Very fair most of the time
    2______Sometimes fair, sometimes not fair
    3______Hardly ever fair

11. Do you think the top officials and bosses of the company are fair to the workers?
 1______Very fair most of the time
 2______Sometimes fair, sometimes not fair
 3______Hardly ever fair
 4______I don't know because I never have any contact with any of them
12. Do you think there are too many union meetings, too few, or about the right number?
 1______Too many 2______About the right number 3______Too few
13. About how many union meetings have you personally attended in the past year?
 ______________meetings
14. About how many union meetings have you missed during the past year?
 ______________meetings
 Why did you miss them?____
 ____
15. About how often do you speak up at a union meeting?
 1______Usually several times a meeting
 2______Once a meeting on the average
 3______Only once in a while
 4______Practically never
16. Do you get a chance to say what you think in union meetings?
 1______Yes, get a good chance
 2______Get a chance if I try hard
 3______No, get no chance
17. Would you rather go to a union meeting or would you rather spend your time doing something else like going to a good movie or playing cards?
 1______Would rather go to a union meeting than to almost anything else
 2______Sometimes rather go to union meetings; sometimes something else
 3______Would rather do something else that I like to do
18. In addition to having regular business taken up at the union meetings, would you like to have discussions, outside speakers, labor and political movies, or singing? (If "yes," ask which.)
 1______Nothing extra
 2______Discussions
 3______Outside speakers
 4______Labor and political movies
 5______Singing
 6______Other (What? ____
 ____)
19. Do you think it would have been better to have remained a CIO union, or is it better to have become an AF of L union, or doesn't it make any difference providing you have a good local union?
 1______Better to have stayed in CIO
 2______Better to be in AF of L
 3______Doesn't make any difference provided the local union is good
 4______Don't know
20. Why do you think your local union broke from the Retail and Wholesale Workers Union, CIO, in the first place a little over a year ago?____________
 ____
 ____
 ____

21. Why do you think your local union joined the Teamsters Union, AF of L, a few months ago?____________________________________

22. Do union problems which do *not* concern your shop interest you? (If asked "What do you mean?" say, "Like getting more members, labor politics.")
1_____Yes, very much
2_____Yes, somewhat
3_____No, only very occasionally
4_____No, not at all

23. Why? ____________________________________

24. If your union is strong enough, will it always be able to get wage increases, or will there come a time soon when the employer can't afford wage increases?
1_____Yes, the union can get anything if it works hard enough
2_____No, there is a limit to what the employer can or will pay
3_____Depends on how business conditions are and whether prices go up some more
4_____Don't know

25. The last time your shop was negotiating a contract, were the workers in your shop strongly behind your negotiating committee?
1_____Yes, very strongly
2_____Yes, rather strongly
3_____No, not very strongly
4_____Hardly any support at all

26. What do you think are the *main things* your union should work for right now, either through collective bargaining or through social action in the community? ____________________________________

27. Why did you join the union?____________________________________

28. Since you are a member of a union, do you feel that your boss can't push you around as much as he might want to?
1_____Yes, he can't push me around
2_____No, the union hardly helps at all
3_____The union helps some, but not completely

29. Do you think promotions and layoffs should be made on the basis of strict seniority?
1_____Yes, always on a basis of seniority
2_____No, on some other basis (What?____________________)
3_____Sometimes on a basis of seniority, sometimes on some other basis (What and when?____________________)

30. Have you read the agreement (the contract) between your union and your company?

_____Yes 1_____No

(If "yes") How much of it do you understand?

2_____All of it
3_____Most of it
4_____Some of it
5_____Little or none of it

31. From what you know of the agreement (the contract), is it a good one, a bad one, or just average?
1_____Good 2_____Bad 3_____Average
32. Is it just as wrong for a worker to file a grievance which is not permitted by his contract as it is for a boss to break a contract?
1_____Yes 2_____No 3_____It depends (on what? ____________________________________)
33. How much time and money should your union put into organizing workers in places where there is no union now?
1_____A great deal
2_____Some
3_____Very little
4_____None at all
34. Should your union put more time and money into unionizing these nonunion places or should it put more into getting more and better things for the people already in the union?
1_____More into new organizational drives
2_____More into working for present union members
3_____About same amount
35. Do you think the union should put more time and money into getting higher wages from the employers, or should it put more into a health plan, social and recreational activities, an insurance plan, and other things of that kind?
1_____More into higher wages 3_____About same amount
2_____More into other things
36. How much time and money should your union put into getting candidates elected to public office who are friendly to labor?
1_____A great deal 3_____Very little
2_____Some 4_____None at all
37. During an election year, how much money would you be willing to give in order to help candidates friendly to labor?______________________________
38. Did you vote in the 1948 election for President? _____Yes 1_____No
(If "yes") Would you mind saying for whom you voted?
2_____Truman
3_____Dewey
4_____Thomas
5_____Wallace
6________________
7_____Won't say
39. Did your wife (husband) vote in the 1948 election for President?
1_____Yes 2_____No 3_____No spouse

Should the union engage in politics in any of the following ways?

	1	2
40. Tell members which candidates are friendly to labor	_____Yes	_____No
41. Advise members how to vote	_____Yes	_____No
42. Help to start a Labor party sometime in the future	_____Yes	_____No

43. Get union members to run for political office ______Yes______No
44. Encourage union members to go to the polls ______Yes______No
45. Collect a dollar from each union member to help friendly candidates ______Yes______No
46. Spend union funds to get laws friendly to labor ______Yes______No
47. How often do you read the *Midwest Labor World*?
1______Twice a month (every issue) 3______Once in a while
2______Once a month (every other issue) 4______Seldom or never
48. What parts of it do you usually read?
1______Headline story 6______Labor Health Bulletin
2______Front-page news 7______Back-page news
3______Editorials 8______Advertisements
4______News from the Shops 9______Other______
5______Stein Shift
49. What parts do you usually skip?
1______Headline story 6______Labor Health Bulletin
2______Front-page news 7______Back-page news
3______Editorials 8______Advertisements
4______News from the Shops 9______Other______
5______Stein Shift
50. Is there anything you would like to see in the *Midwest Labor World* which is not there now?______
______
______
51. Have you ever taken an educational course, such as a leadership class, through your union?
1______No 2______Yes (How many courses?______)
52. Would you like to take an education course now?
1______Yes 2______No 3______Maybe later on
53. (If "yes" or "later on") On what subjects?______
______
54. Suppose your union offered a course on present-day politics, would you take it?
1______Yes 2______No
55. Suppose your union offered a course on labor economics and collective bargaining, would you take it?
1______Yes 2______No
56. Suppose your union offered a course on public speaking, would you take it?
1______Yes 2______No
57. Suppose your union offered a course on minority groups, such as Negroes and Jews, would you take it?
1______Yes 2______No
58. Would you be willing to attend workers' classes outside the city for 3 days to 2 weeks in the summer – like the schools at Madison and Montebello?
1______Yes, very much 3______No, not interested
2______Yes, might consider it 4______Don't know

(All questions on Negroes to be asked of whites only)

59. Do you think it is a good idea or a bad idea for your union to try to get Negroes into jobs in the place where you work when there are vacancies?
1______Good idea 3______O.K. up to a point
2______Bad idea
60. Do you think it is a good idea or a bad idea for your union to try to get

Negroes into all kinds of jobs in the place, including good jobs, when there are vacancies and Negroes have seniority?

1______Good idea 3______O.K. up to a point
2______Bad idea

61. Do you think that Negroes should be permitted to live in the same block with white persons?
1______Yes 2______No

62. Do you think that Negroes should be permitted to live in the same building with white persons?
1______Yes 2______No

63. Would you object to Negro and white children going to the same school?
1______Yes 2______No

64. Do you think that when the union has parties, picnics, and dances, there should be separate ones for Negroes, or should Negroes be invited to the same social affairs with whites?
1______Separate for Negroes
2______Negroes and whites at same affairs
3______Negroes should be allowed to come, but not encouraged
4______Don't care either way

65. Have your attitudes toward Negroes changed since you became a member of the union?
______Yes 1______No
(If "yes") How so?
2______Much more friendly 5______Much less friendly
3______Somewhat more friendly 6______Don't know
4______Somewhat less friendly

66. Have your attitudes toward Jews changed since you became a member of the union?
______Yes 1______No
(If "yes") How so?
2______Much more friendly 5______Much less friendly
3______Somewhat more friendly 6______Don't know
4______Somewhat less friendly

67. Do you think the union spends too much time, not enough time, or about the right amount of time, on matters affecting Negroes and other minority groups?
1______Not enough time 3______About the right amount
2______Too much time 4______Don't know

68. Do you think union dues are too high, too low, or about right?
1______Too high 3______Too low
2______About right 4______No opinion

69. In addition to dues, the union sometimes asks for assessments and extra payments. Does your union ask for too many extras?
1______Yes, too many extras 2______No, about the right amount of extras

70. Do you think the union should fine members when they don't attend meetings, provided they don't have a legitimate excuse?
1______Yes, they should be fined
2______No, they should not be fined 3______Don't know

71. How often should your union use the strike to get what it wants?
1______Practically never 3______As often as needed
2______Once in a while 4______Often, to prove power

72. Does your union have too many paid staff members, too few, or about the right number?

1_____Too many 2_____Too few 3_____About the right number

73. Are any of the paid union staff members *not* doing a good job?
    1_____All doing a good job 4_____Most doing a poor job
    2_____Most doing a good job 5_____All doing a poor job
    3_____About half and half
74. In what way aren't they doing a good job?____________________
    ____
75. Do you think the union staff members are underpaid, overpaid, or paid just right?
    1_____Underpaid 2_____Overpaid 3_____Paid just right

Are there some union staff members who:

76. are too radical? 1_____Yes 2_____No
77. are too conservative? 1_____Yes 2_____No
78. are too smart? 1_____Yes 2_____No
79. are too dumb? 1_____Yes 2_____No
80. are too ambitious? 1_____Yes 2_____No
81. are too lazy? 1_____Yes 2_____No
82. are too bossy? 1_____Yes 2_____No
83. don't carry through on the job? 1_____Yes 2_____No
84. Do you think the union staff members' conduct is what it should be? (Do they behave properly?)
    1_____Yes _____No 2_____Don't know
    (If "no") In what way?
    3_____No, drinking 6_____No (other:____________________
    4_____No, swearing ____________________)
    5_____No, gambling
85. What do you think of having staff members who come from outside St. Louis?
    1_____Good idea 3_____Don't care either way
    2_____Bad idea
86. What do you think of having women on the union staff?
    1_____Good idea 2_____Bad idea 3_____Don't care either way
87. What do you think of having Jews on the union staff?
    1_____Good idea 2_____Bad idea 3_____Don't care either way
88. What do you think of having Negroes on the union staff?
    1_____Good idea 2_____Bad idea 3_____Don't care either way

Do you agree or disagree with the following statements?

89. It would be a good idea if more business concerns would refuse to hire Jews.
    1_____Agree 2_____Disagree 3_____Can't decide
90. It would be a good idea to keep Jews out of Christian neighborhoods.
    1_____Agree 2_____Disagree 3_____Can't decide
91. It would be a good idea if Jews were prevented from getting more power in the business world.
    1_____Agree 2_____Disagree 3_____Can't decide
92. In general, Jews should not be allowed to hold high political office.
    1_____Agree 2_____Disagree 3_____Can't decide
93. In general, Catholics should not be allowed to hold high political office.
    1_____Agree 2_____Disagree 3_____Can't decide
94. Negroes should be put on separate jobs from whites.
    1_____Agree 2_____Disagree 3_____Can't decide
95. Do you dislike working side by side with a Jew, doing the same kind of work?
    1_____Yes, dislike very much
    2_____Dislike a little, but not seriously
    3_____No, don't dislike at all

96. Do you dislike working side by side with Negroes, doing the same kind of job?
1_____Yes, dislike very much
2_____Dislike a little, but not seriously
3_____No, don't dislike at all

97. Do you think it is a good idea or a bad idea to have Negroes on a picket line along with whites?
1_____Good idea 2_____Doesn't make any difference 3_____Bad idea

98. Would you rather have important matters affecting the union be decided by the union's director, by the stewards' council, or by the rank-and-file members?
1_____By the union's director 3_____By the rank-and-file members
2_____By the stewards' council

99. Who do you think does most of the deciding now?
1_____The union's director 3_____The rank-and-file members
2_____The stewards' council

100. Is it more important that the top leaders of the union get what the members want and need than it is that the union be democratic, or is it more important for the union to be democratic?
1_____More important that the union get what members want and need
2_____More important that the union be democratic
3_____Don't know

101. Have you ever been on a picket line? _____Yes 1_____No
(If "yes") Was it for your own shop or some other shop?
2_____Own shop 3_____Some other shop 4_____Both

102. Have you ever thought of trying to become a union officer or staff member?
1_____Yes, often 2_____Yes, occasionally 3_____No, never

103. Are you willing to picket to help some other shop get organized or get a raise in pay?
1_____Yes 2_____No

104. How does the medical service given by the Labor Health Institute compare with that given by a private doctor?
1_____Better 2_____About the same 3_____Worse

Do you think it is important for the union to have the following services for its members even if some of the cost must come out of the union treasury?

	Yes, very important	Good idea, but not important	No, not important at all
105. Free legal service	1_____	2_____	3_____
106. Free medical and health service	1_____	2_____	3_____
107. Credit union	1_____	2_____	3_____
108. Free employment service	1_____	2_____	3_____

109. In general, is it better to have a woman or a man as a shop steward?
1_____Woman 3_____Makes no difference if person is capable
2_____Man 4_____Depends on whether workers are men or women

110. Does your steward do a good job, fair job, or poor job of handling grievances?
1_____Good job 2_____Fair job 3_____Poor job

111. Do you have any suggestions for improving the handling of grievances?_____
____
____

112. Should wives and husbands of union members be invited to attend regular union meetings?
1_____Yes 2_____No 3_____Don't care either way

113. Should your union have more parties and other social affairs *or* should there be more educational programs?
1_____More social affairs 3_____More of both
2_____More educational programs 4_____Neither
114. What is the best way of organizing these social affairs regarding who should be invited?
1_____Just members of one crew
2_____Just members of one shop
3_____Members from a couple of shops
4_____Members of the same age group regardless of where they work
5_____Anyone in the union who wants to come
115. Do you think your union should have a headquarters with recreational facilities?
1_____No 2_____Yes
(If "yes") With what facilities?____
____
116. Is your family in favor of your belonging to a union?
1_____Yes, they approve strongly 4_____No, they disapprove mildly
2_____Yes, they approve mildly 5_____No, they disapprove strongly
3_____They don't care either way
117. Have any members of your family ever belonged to a union?
1_____No 2_____Yes (Who?____)
118. What kind of union meetings do you like best?
1_____Crew meetings (not over 25 people)
2_____Shop meetings (all people who work for the company)
3_____Meetings of workers in several shops (all people in one industry)
4_____City-wide union meetings (all members of Teamsters Local 688)
5_____No kind of union meeting
119. What chance do you think you have for getting ahead and becoming a foreman or shop owner yourself someday?
1_____No chance at all 3_____Fair chance
2_____Very small chance 4_____Good chance
120. Is there anything else you would like to say about your union?____________
____
____
121. What exactly is your job?____
____
122. How many years have you been a member of the union?____________years
123. Have you ever been a shop steward? 1_____Yes 2_____No
124. How far did you go in school?
1_____Up through 6th grade 4_____Graduated from high school
2_____7th or 8th grade 5_____Some college
3_____Some high school
125. Do you attend church? _____Yes _____No
Regardless of whether or not you attend, what church (denomination) do you favor?____

(Interviewer should guess the answers to the following questions and put in answers *after* he leaves home of respondent.)

126. Age:_____years. 127. Race or nationality:______________
128. Sex:_____Male _____Female
129. Interviewer's estimate of cooperativeness of respondent: _____A _____B _____C _____D _____F

Interviewer's name: (Print)____

Index